I0407991

WONDERFUL DESIGNS AND STRESS RELIEVING PATTERNS

SWEAR TIME!

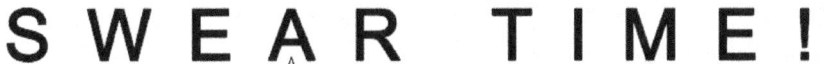

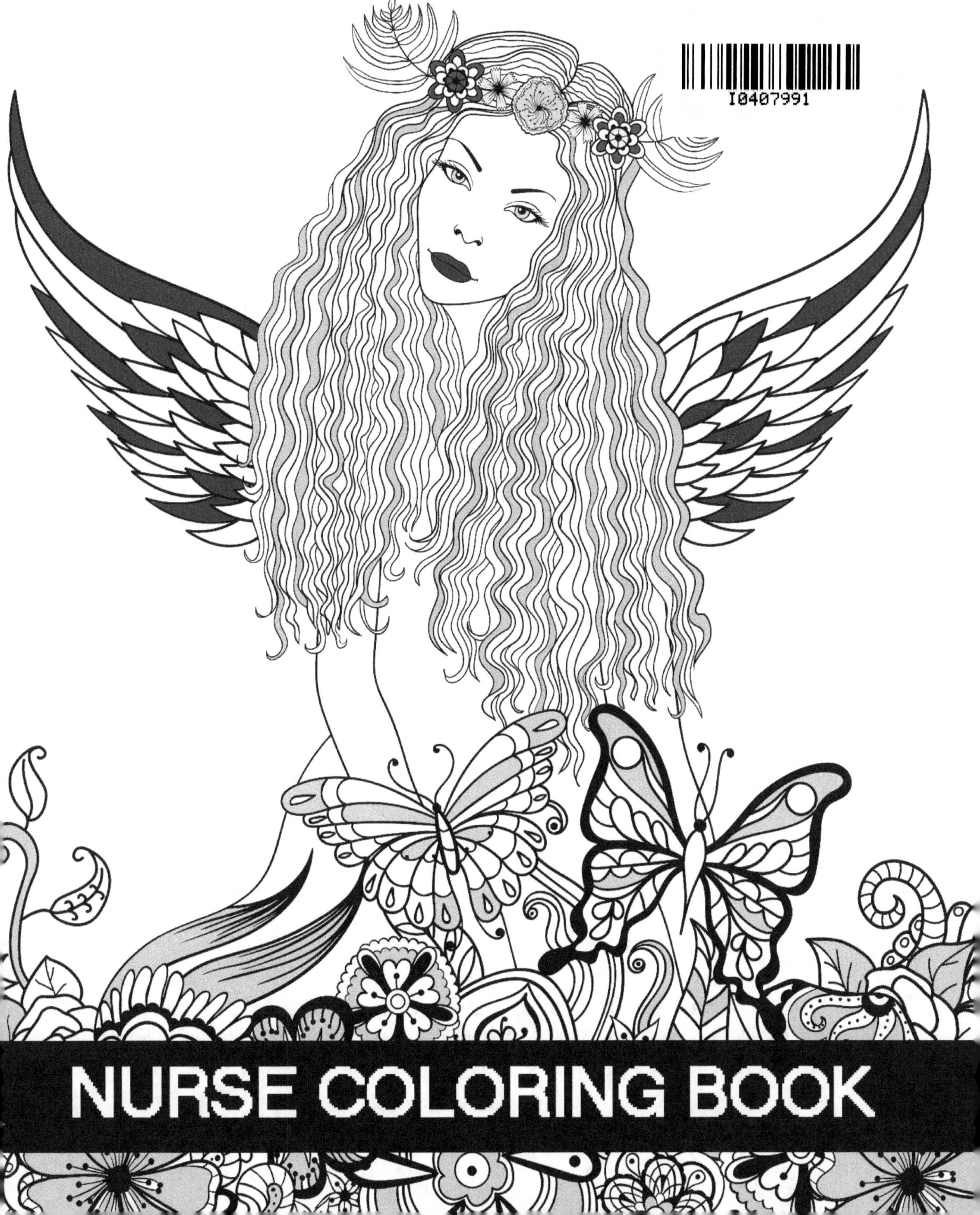

NURSE COLORING BOOK

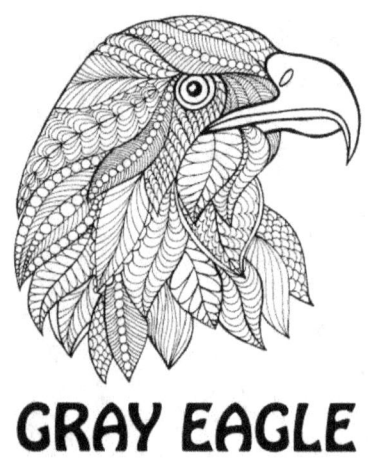

GRAY EAGLE

Copyright 2017

Printed in The U.S.A.

TEST YOUR COLOR

1.

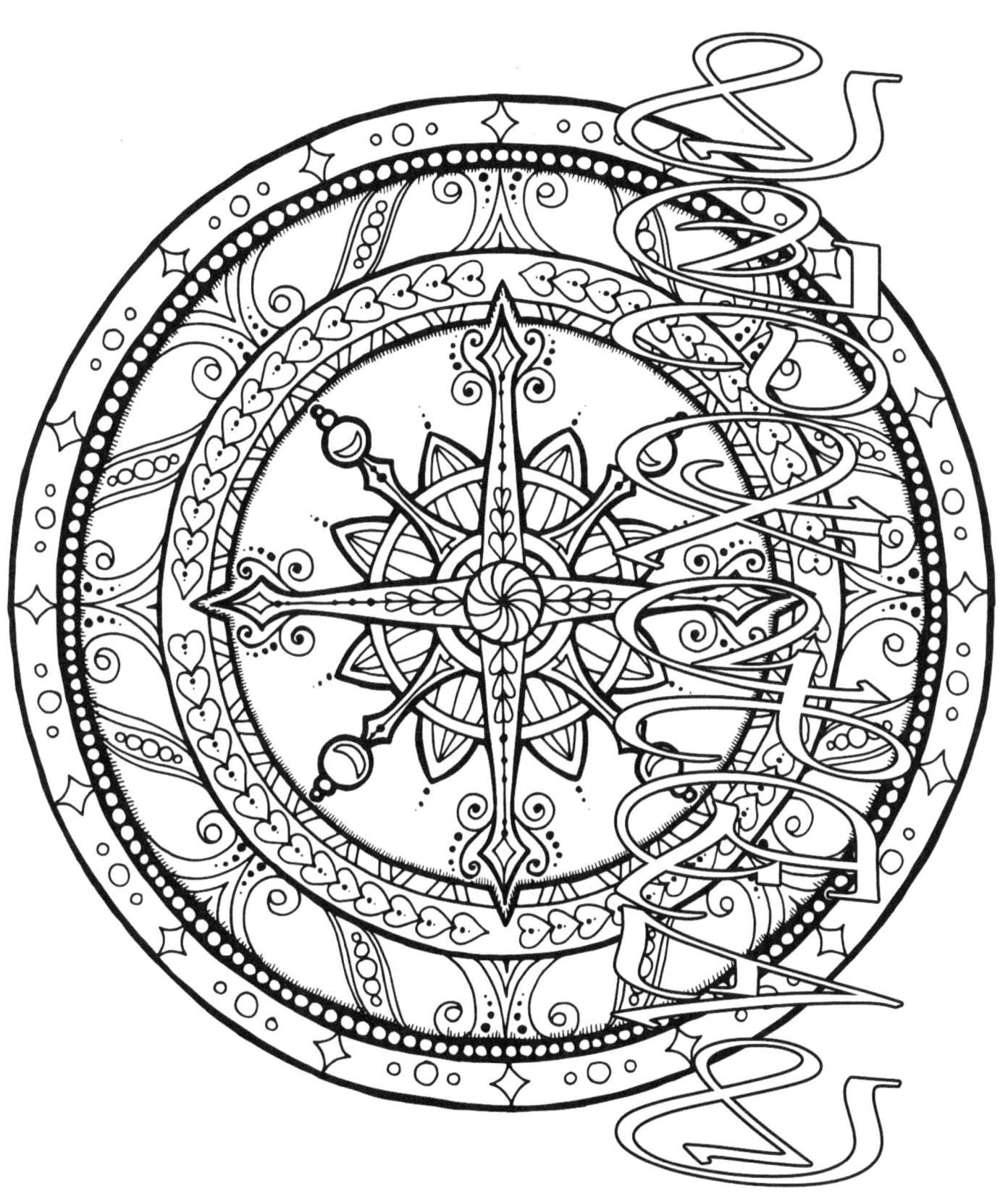

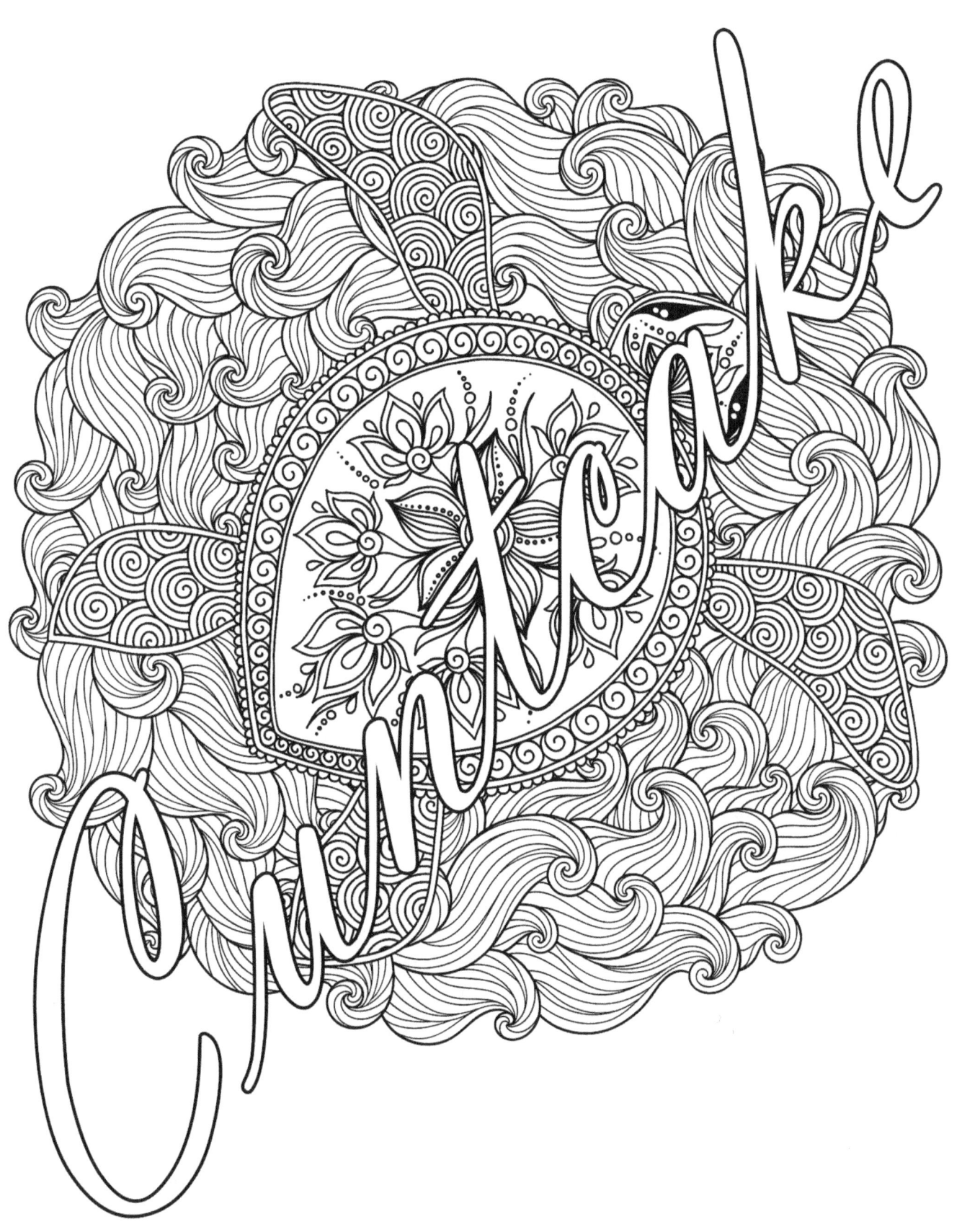

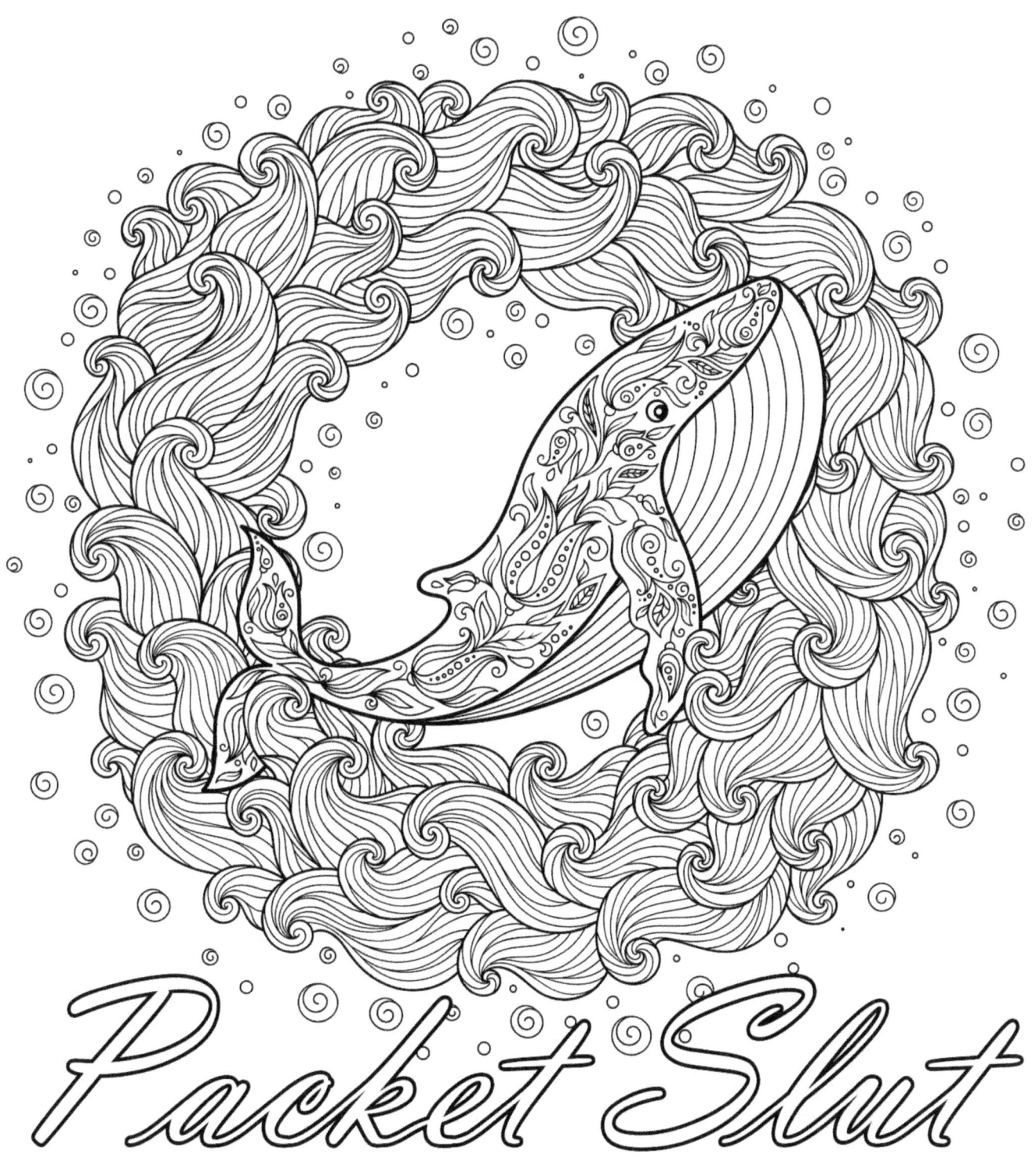

Packet Slut

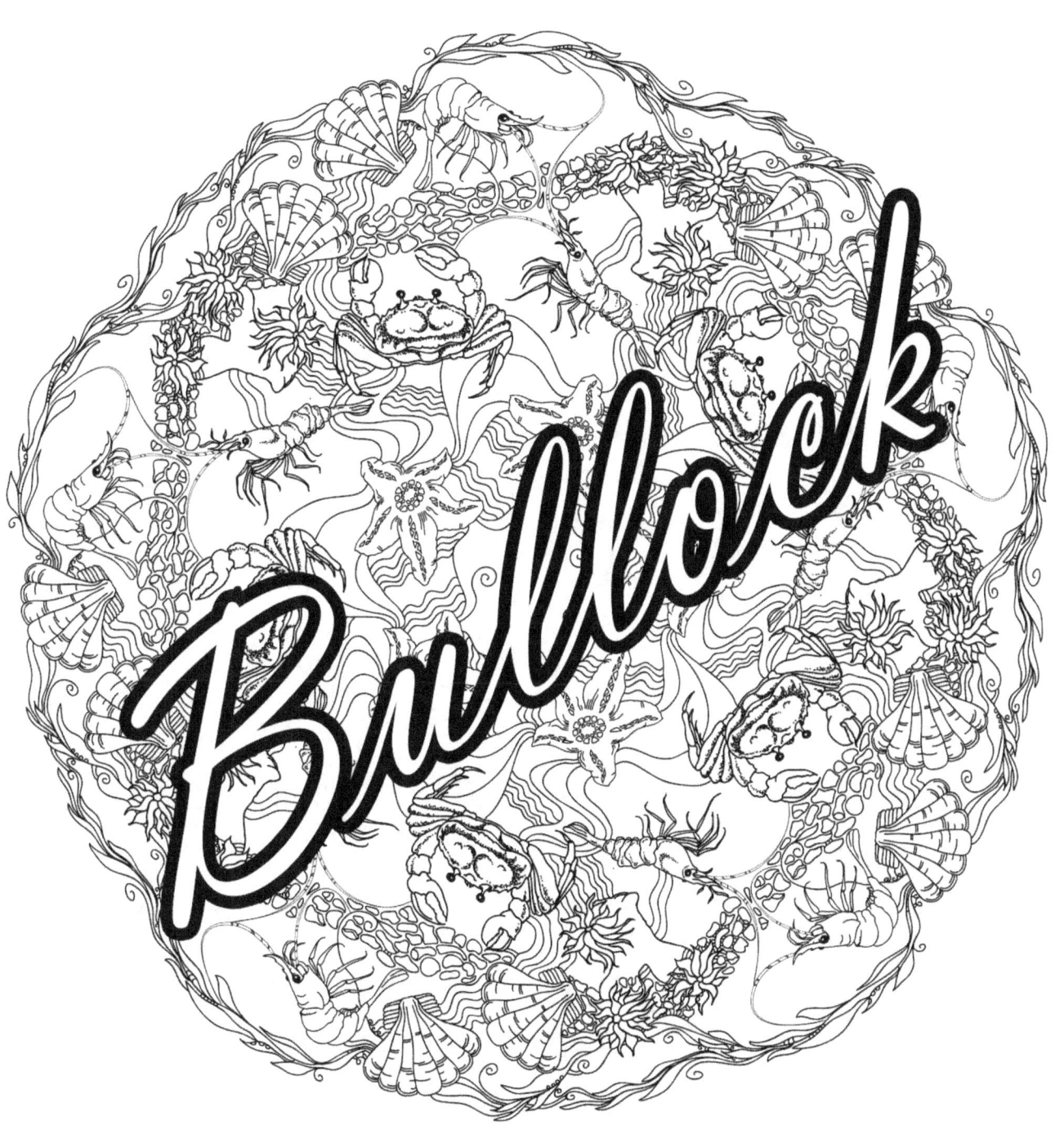

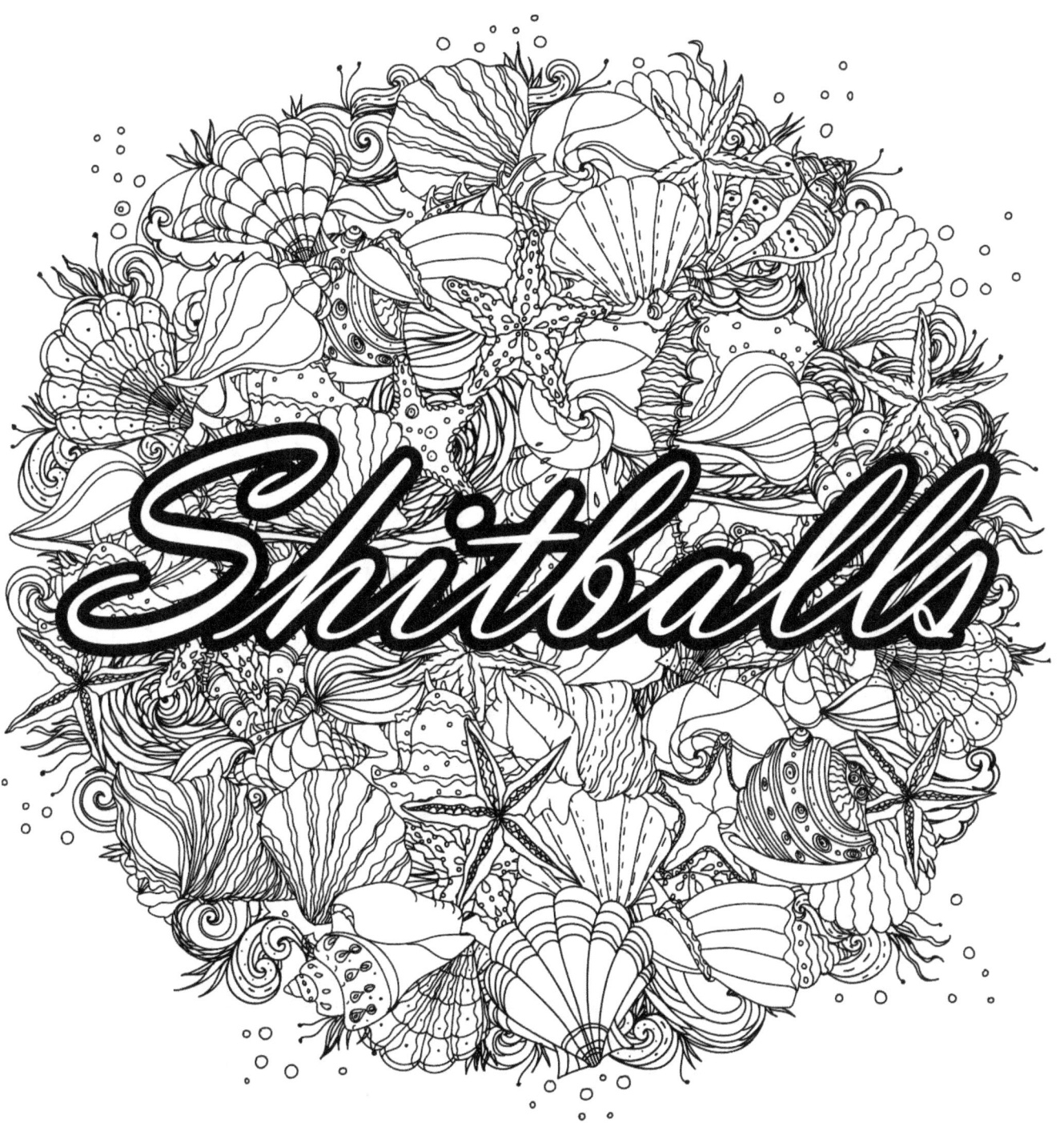

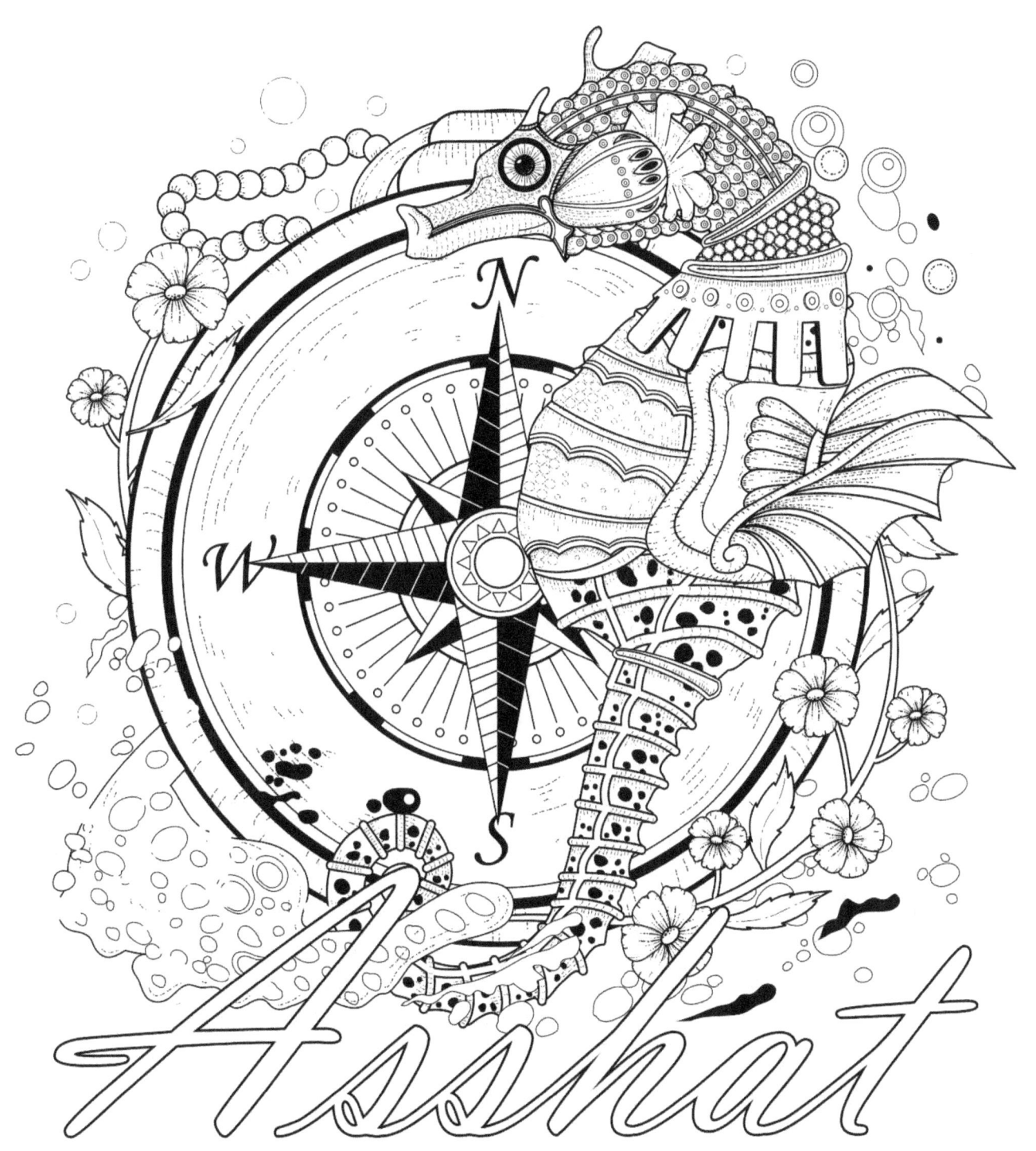

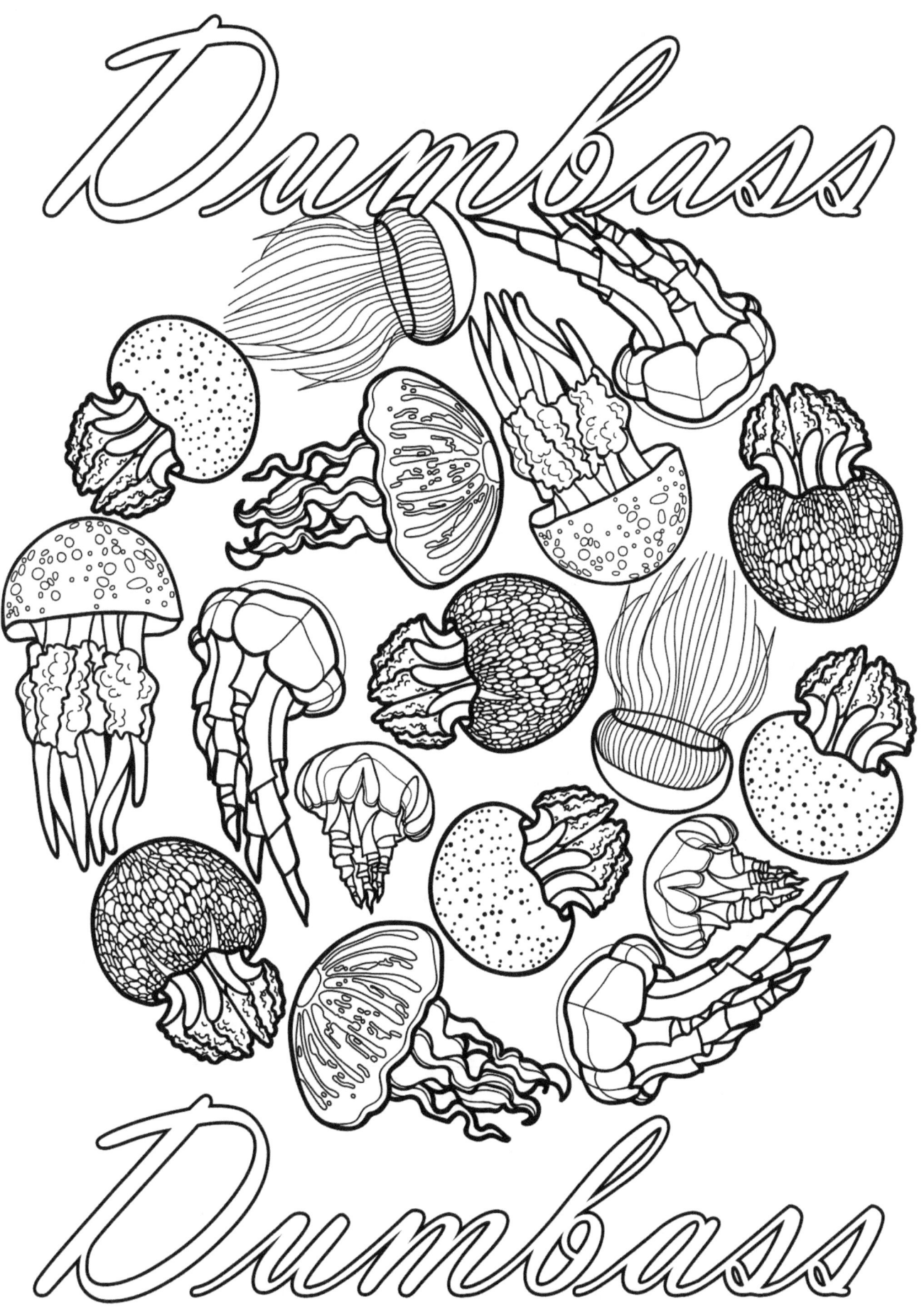

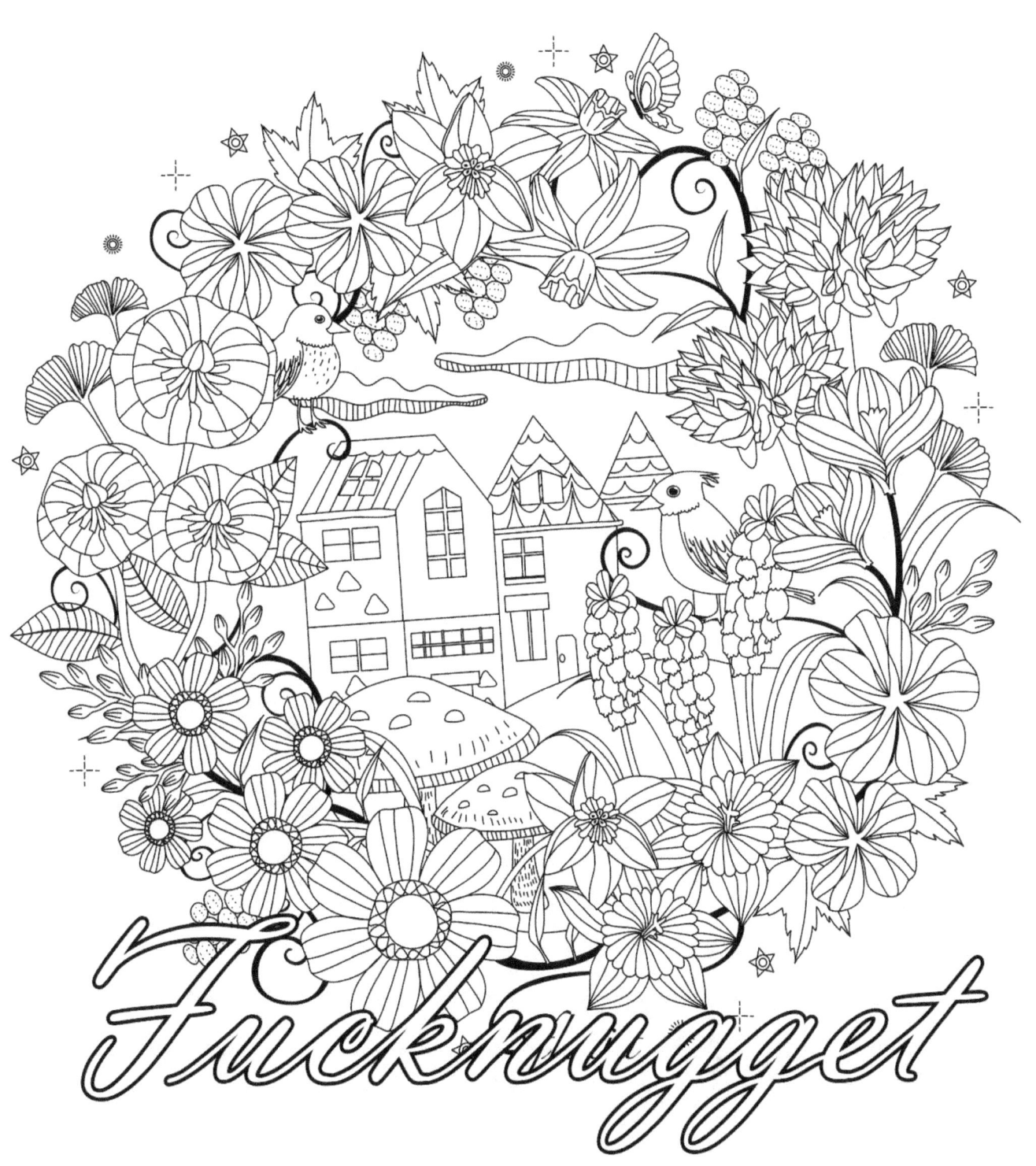

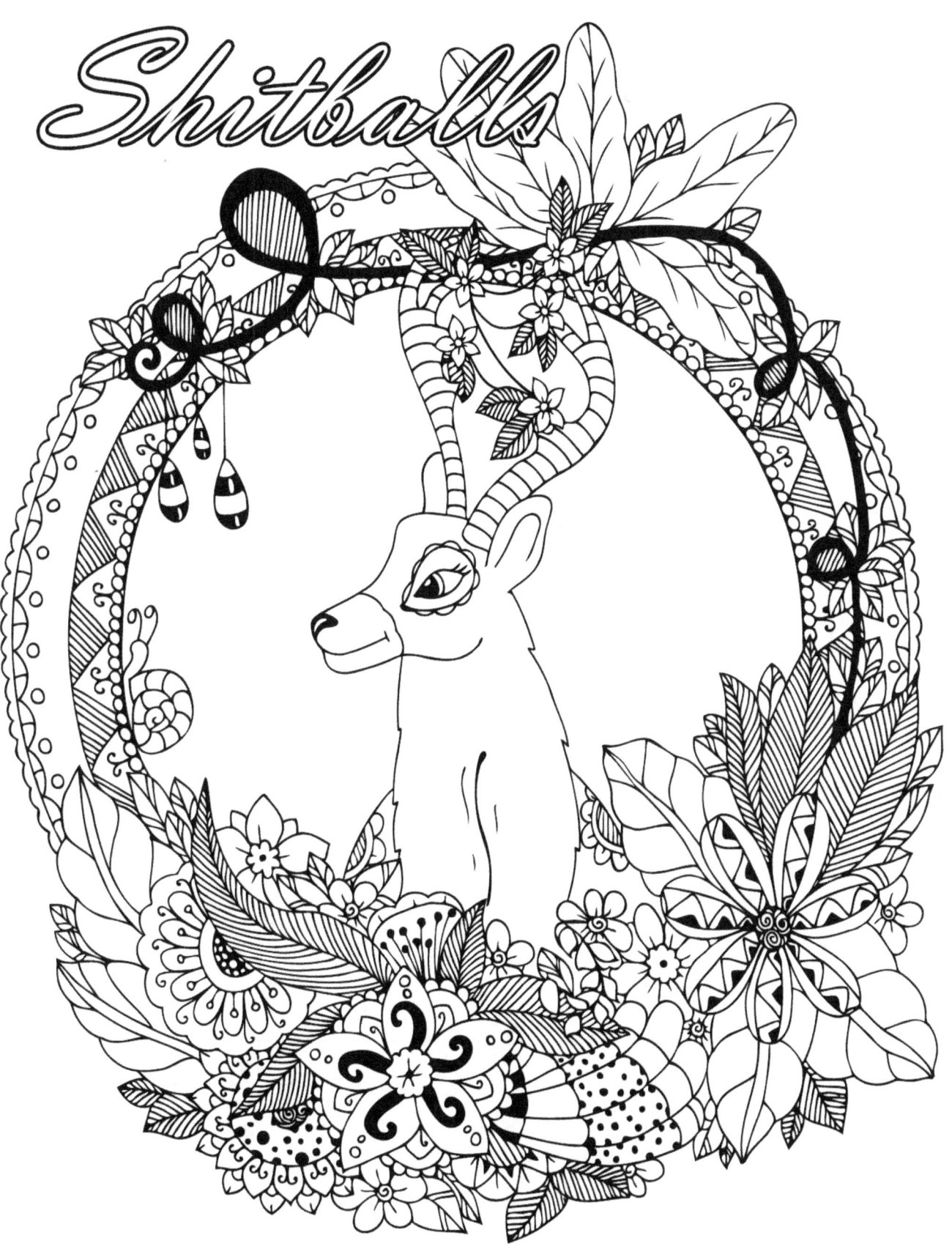

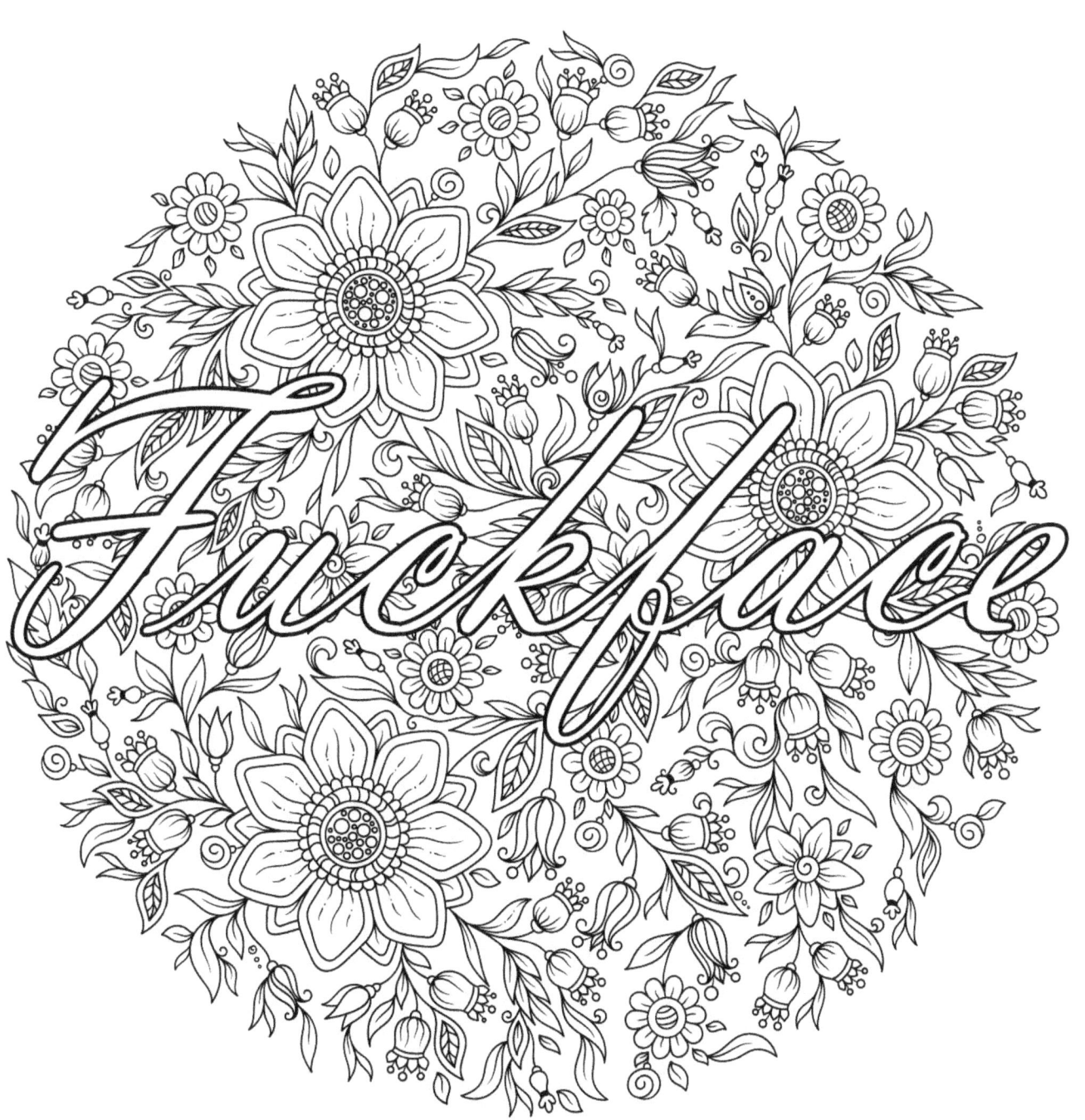

Fuck a Duck

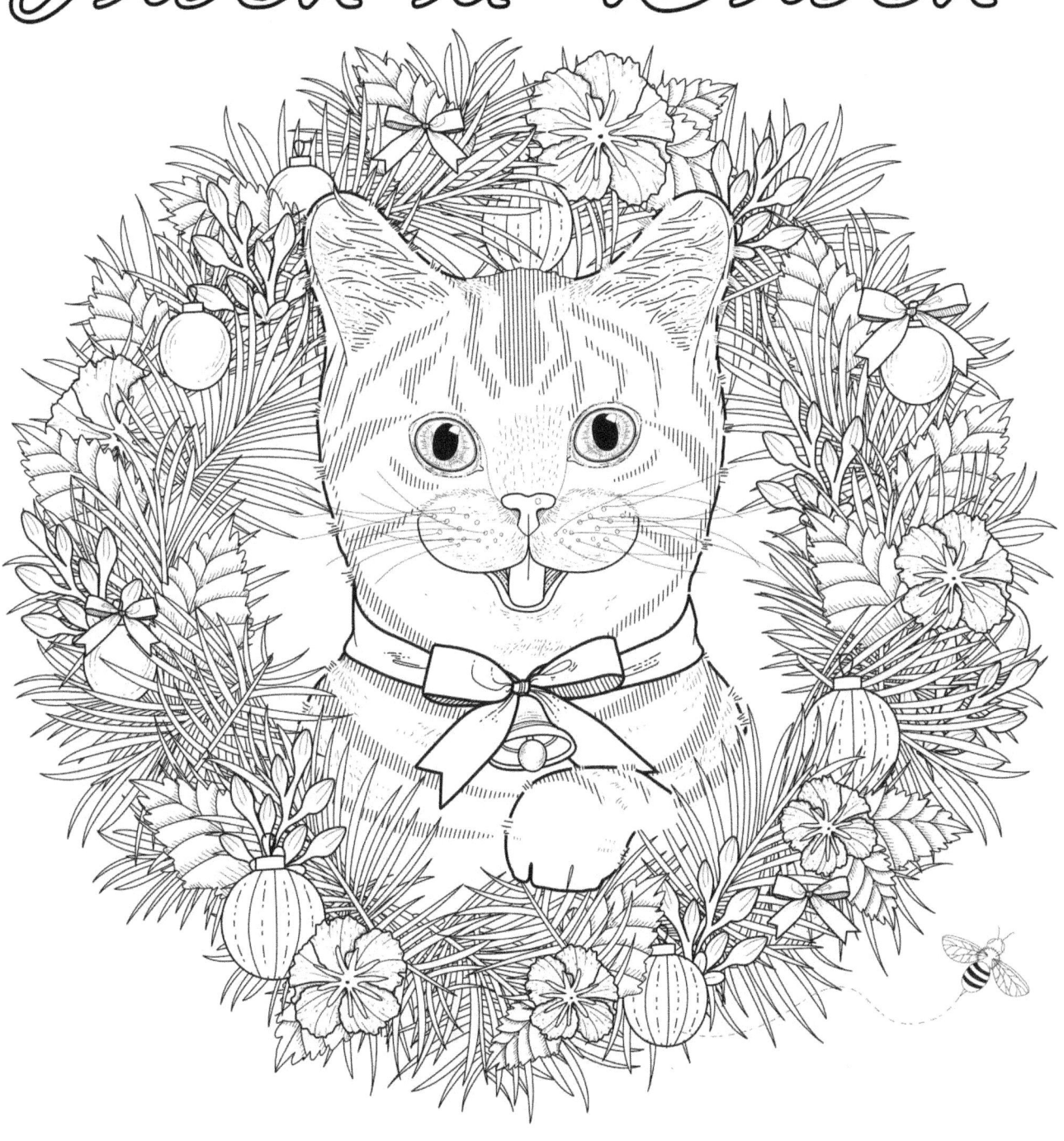

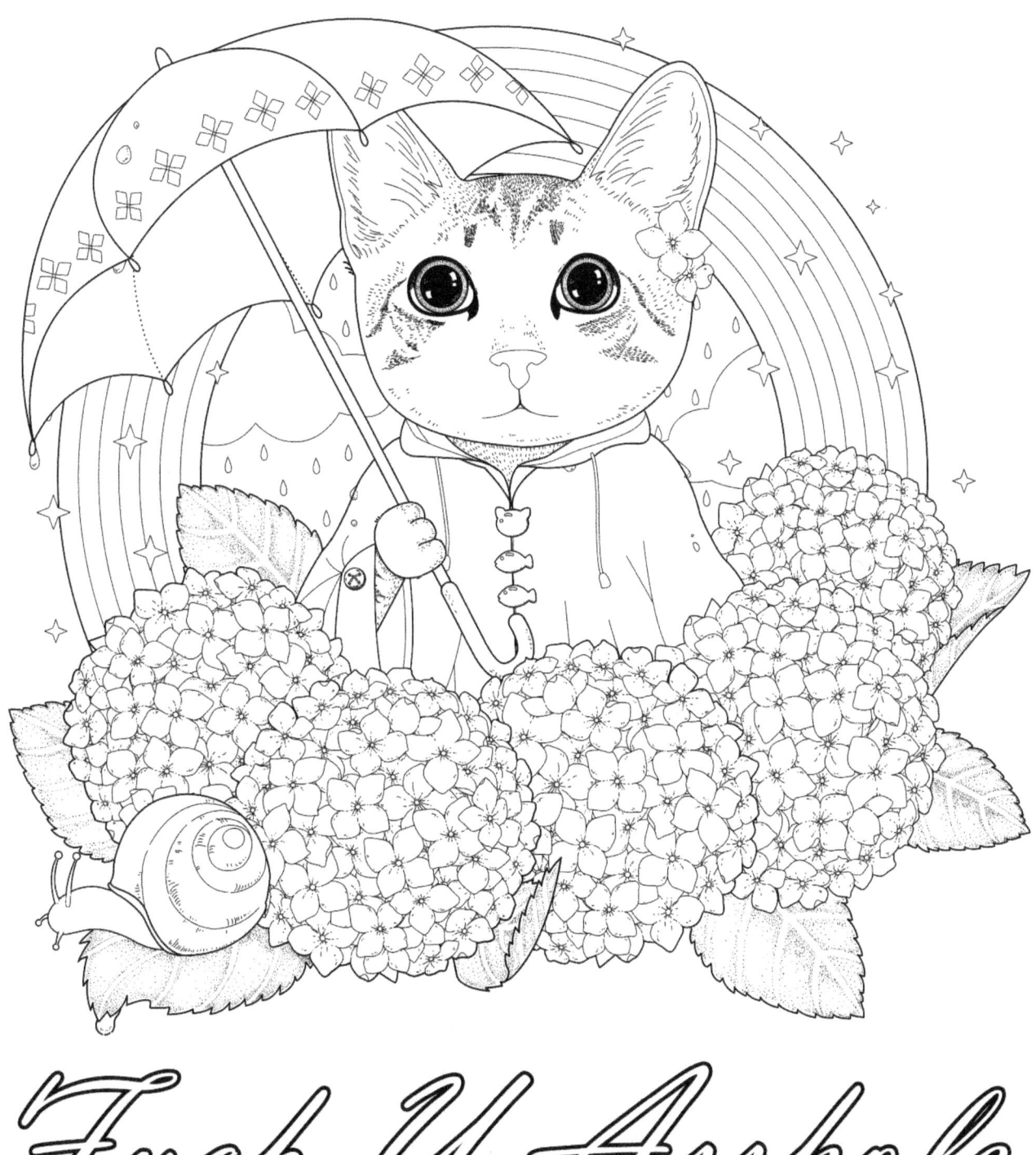

Fuck U Asshole

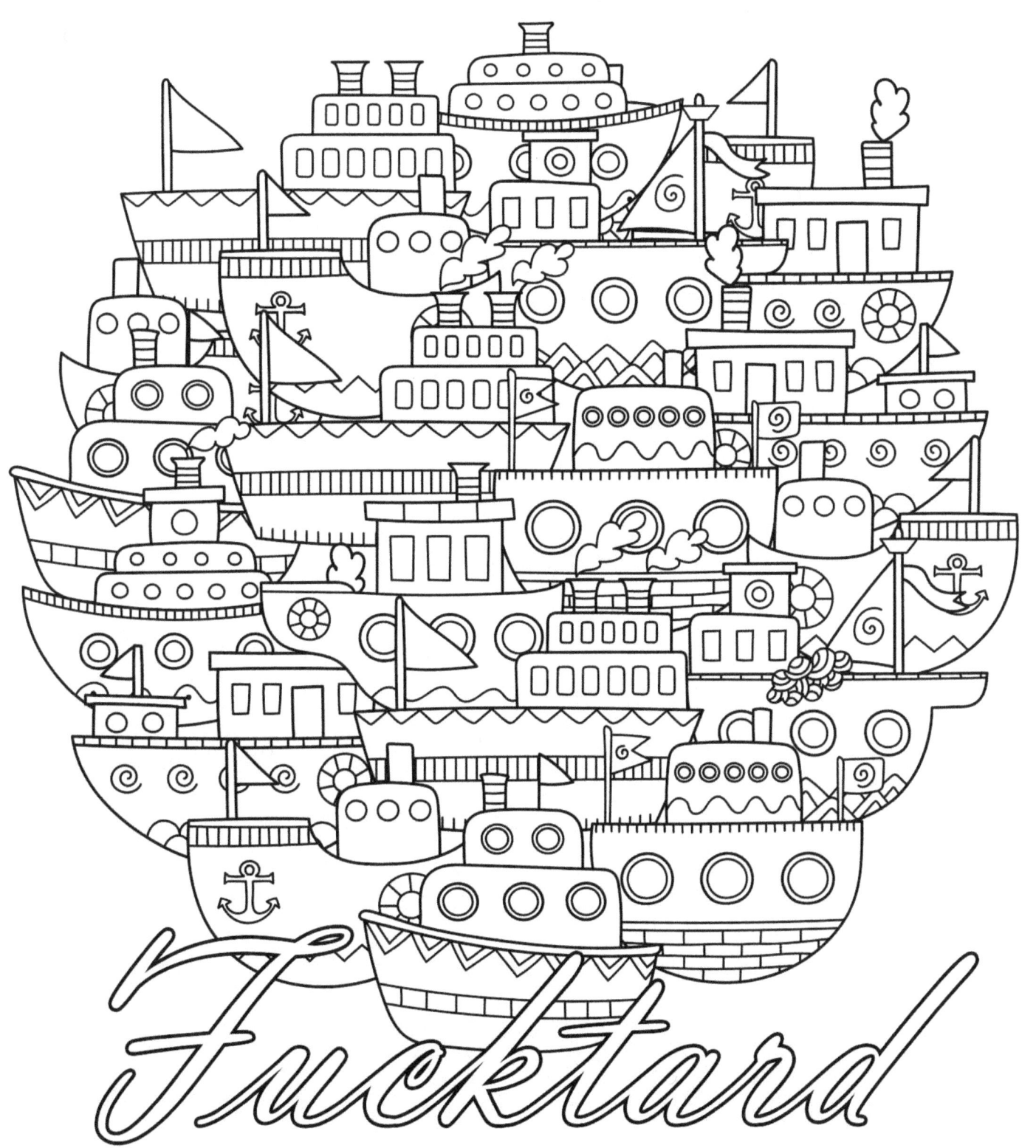

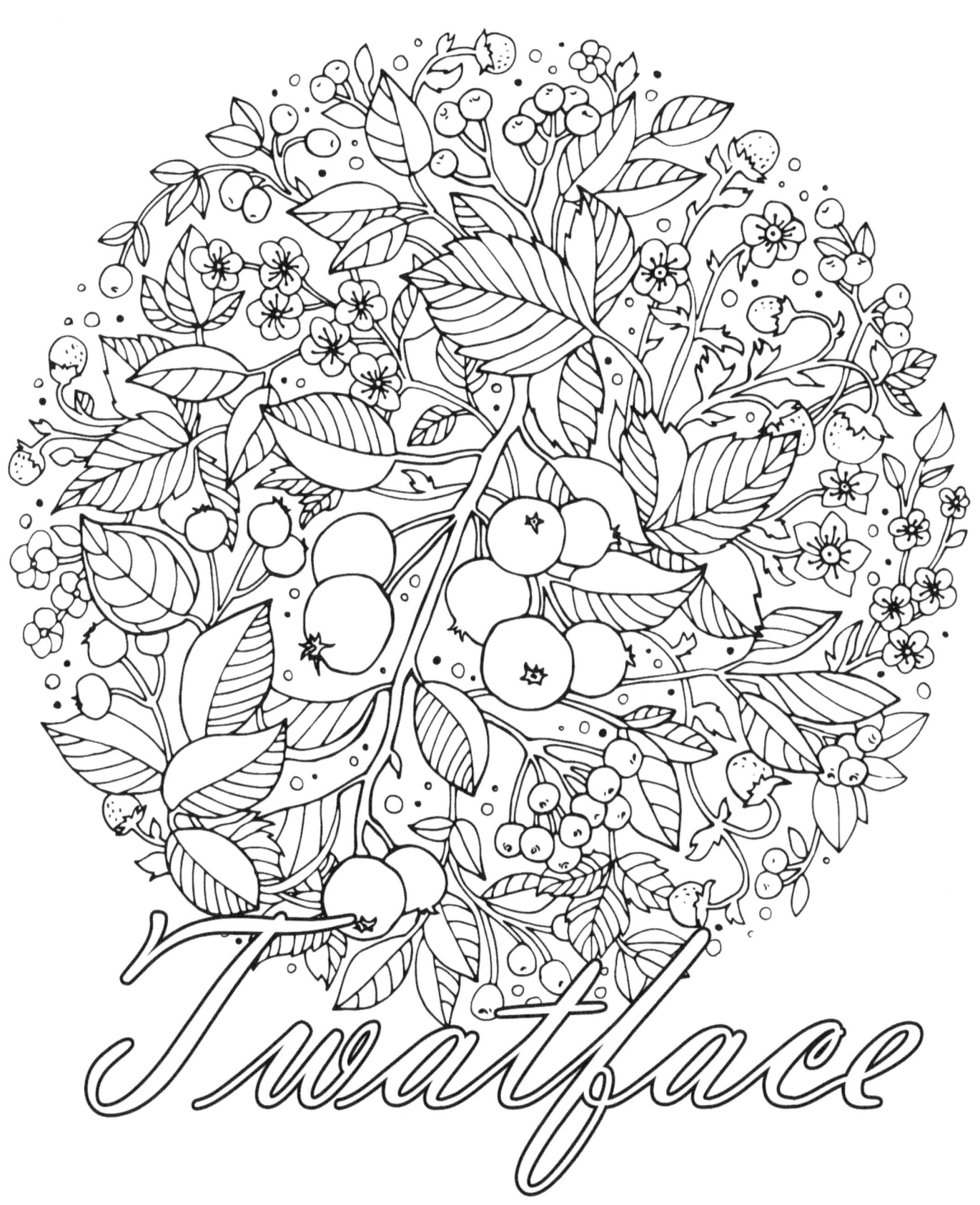

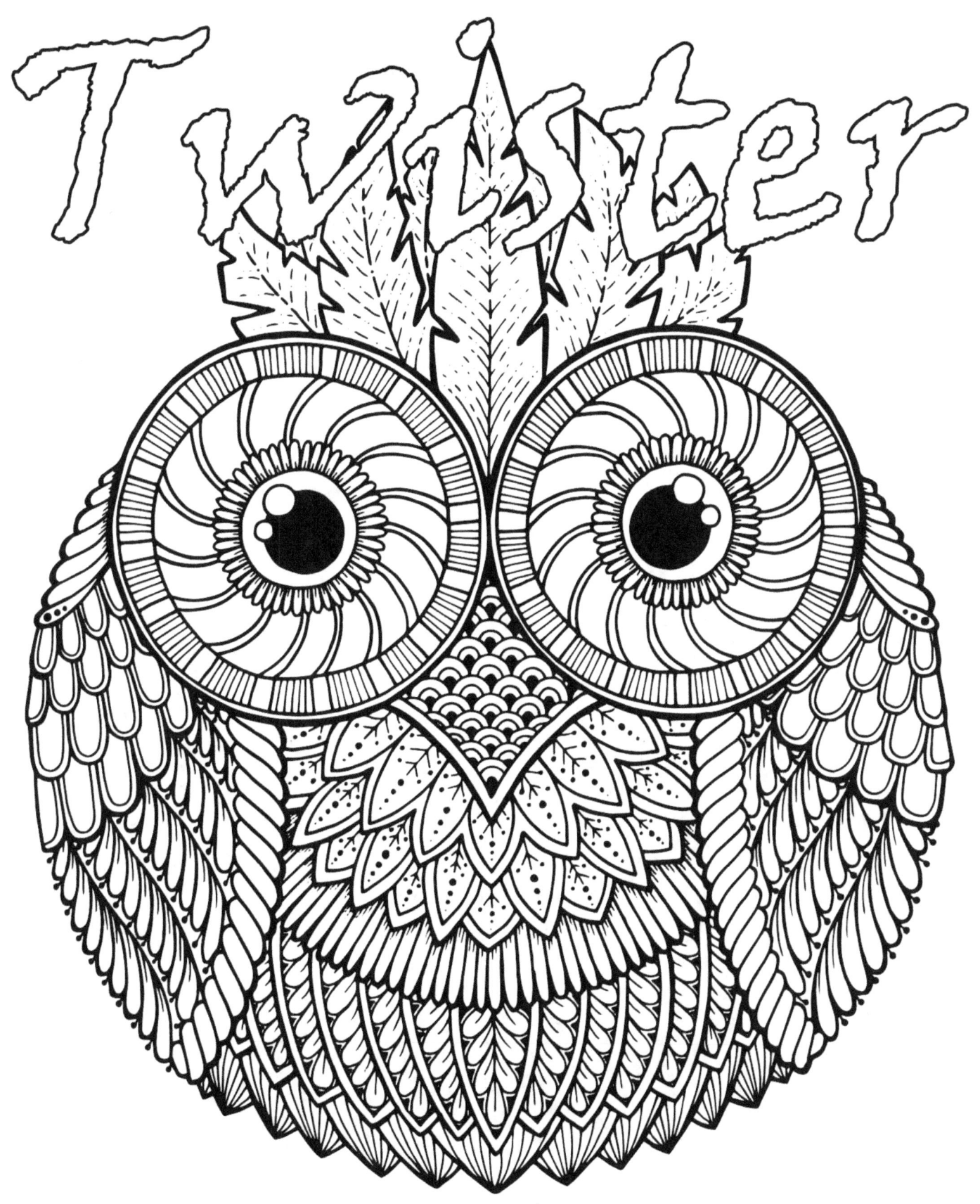

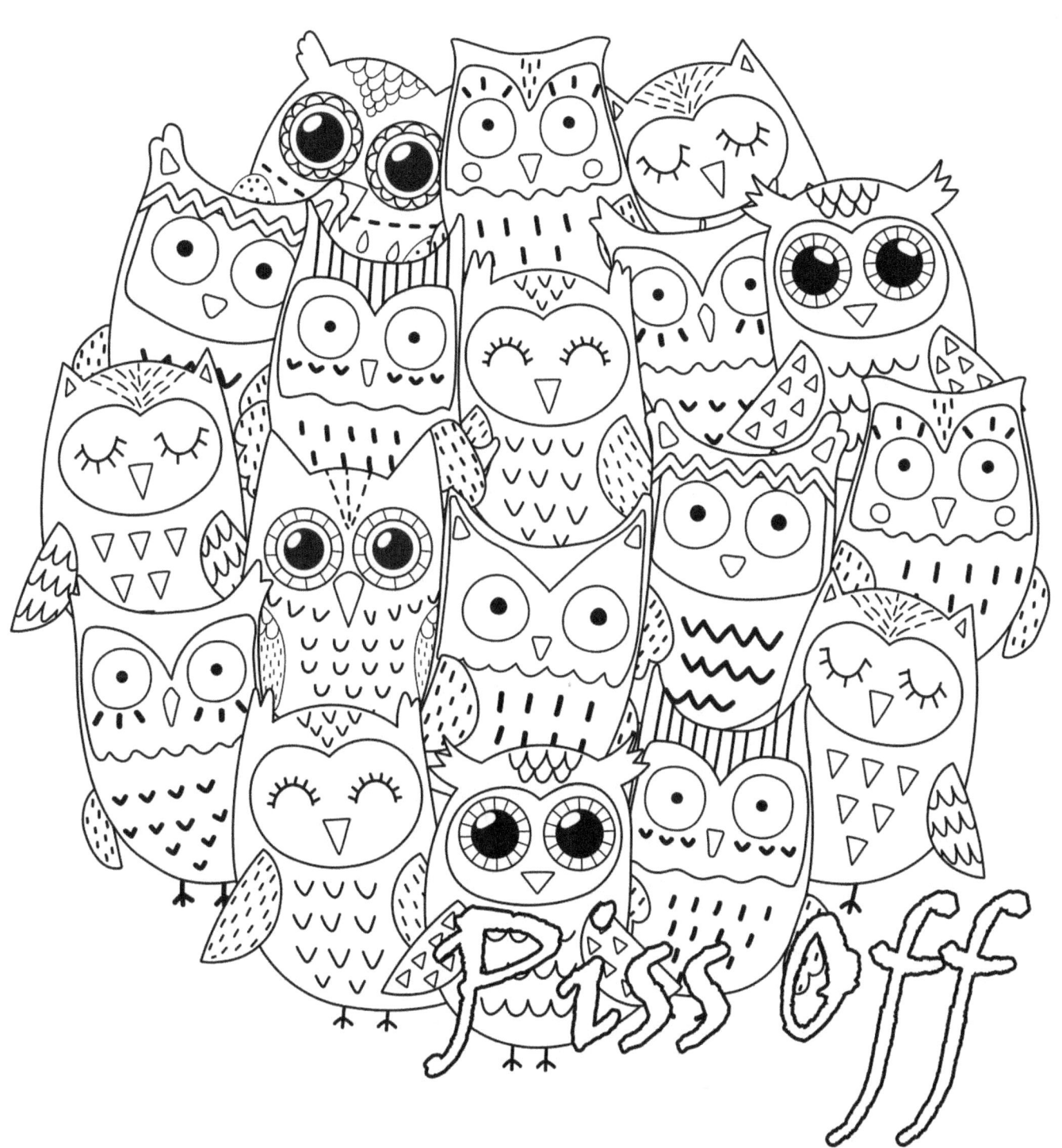

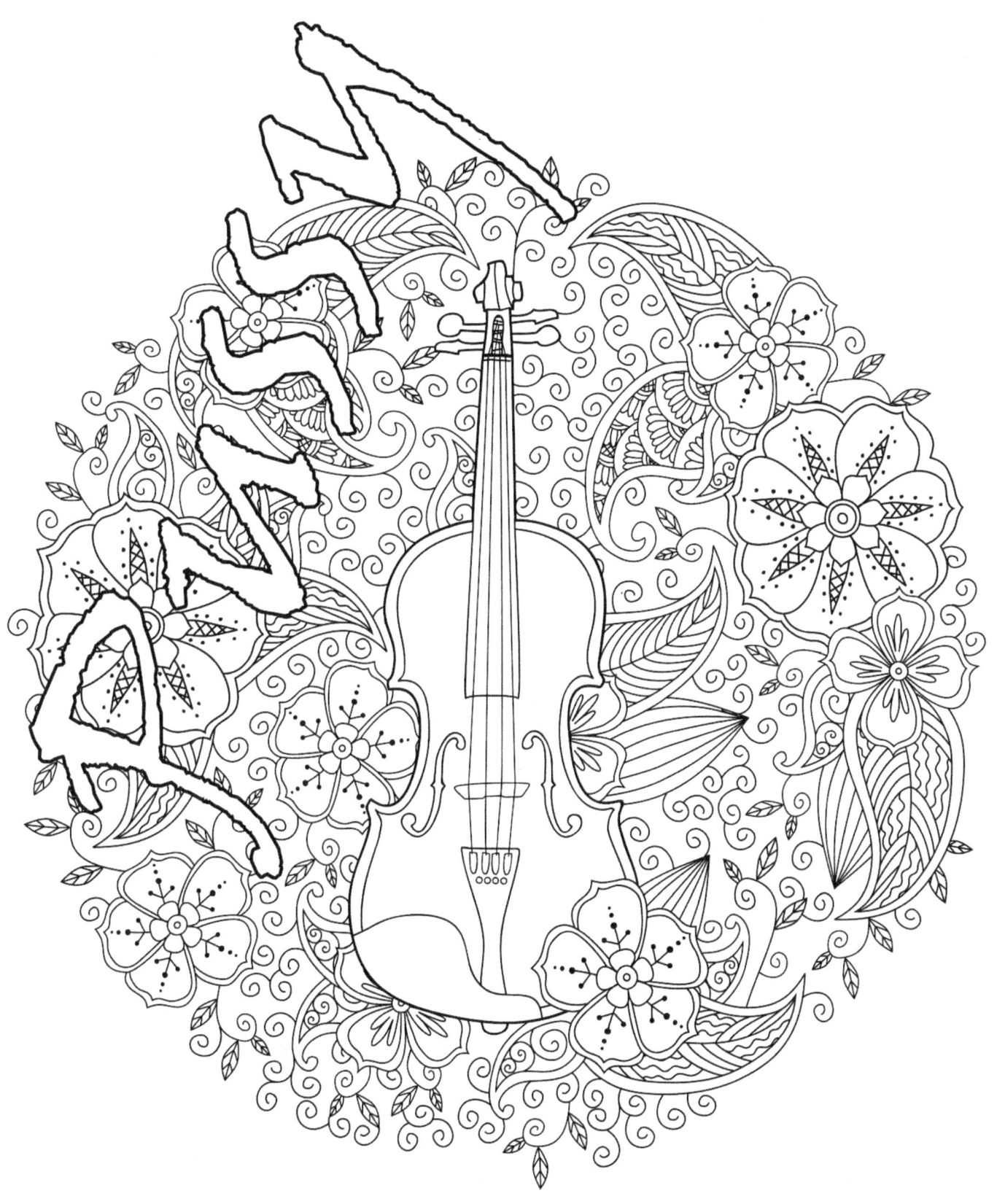

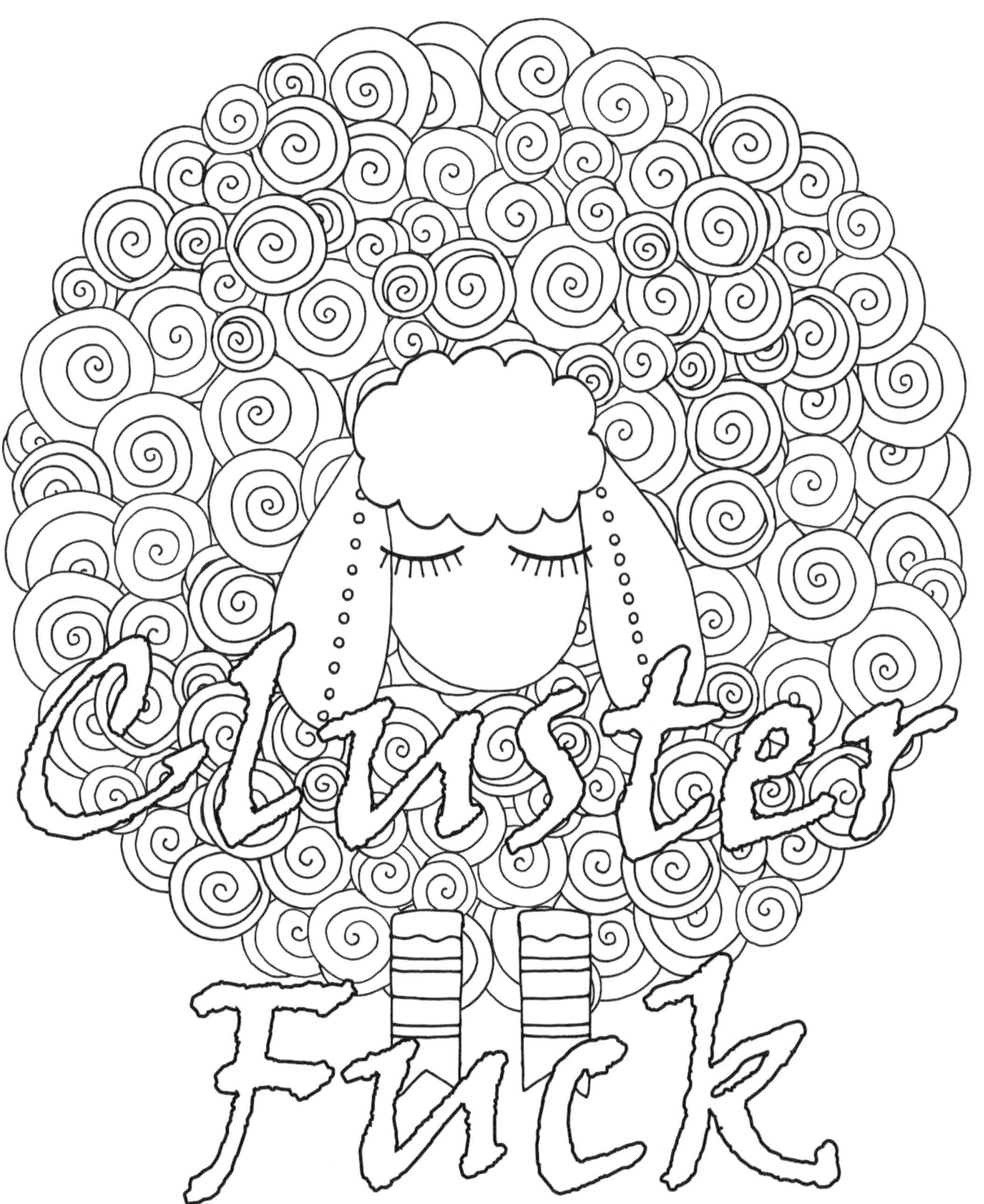

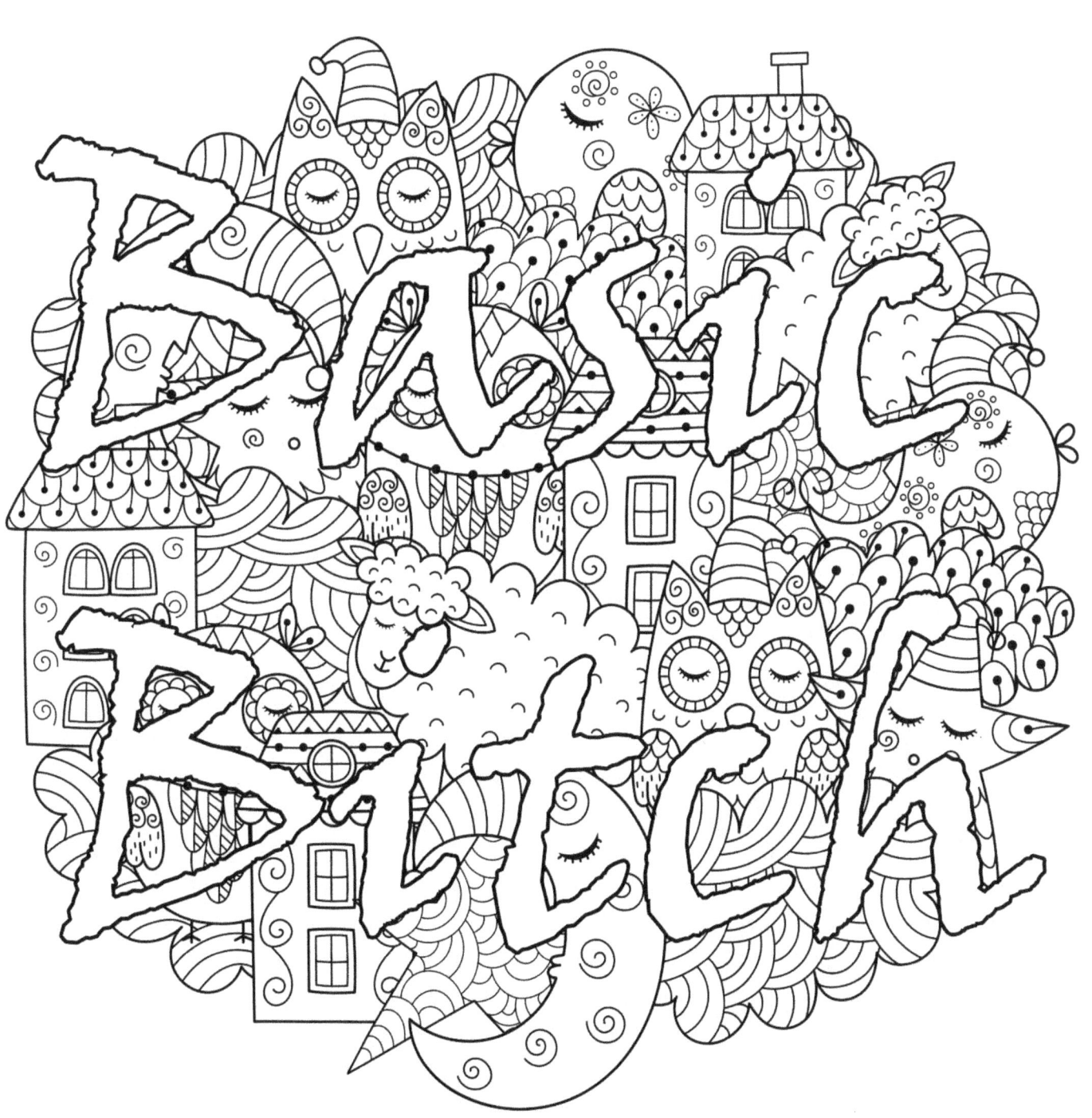

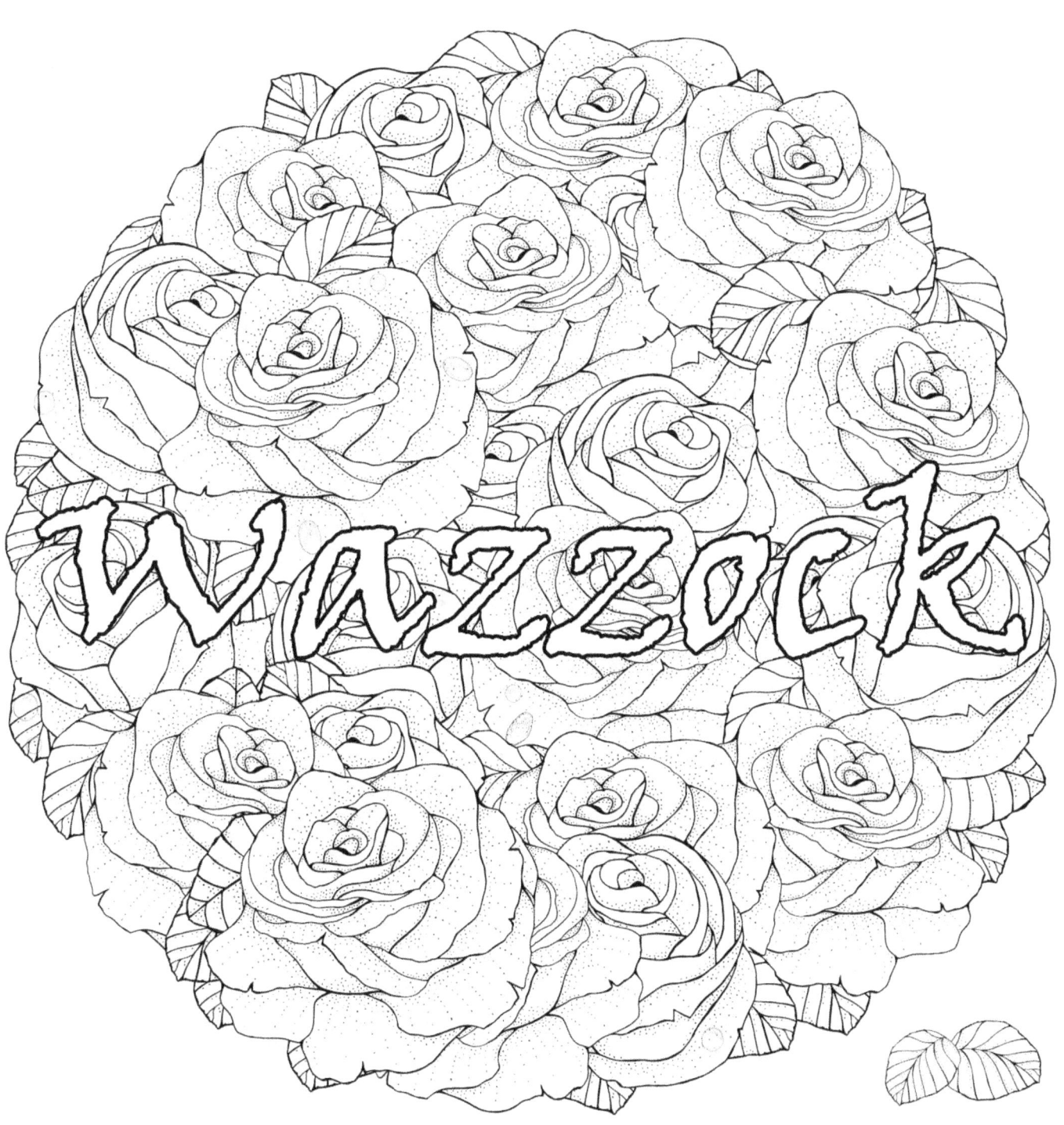

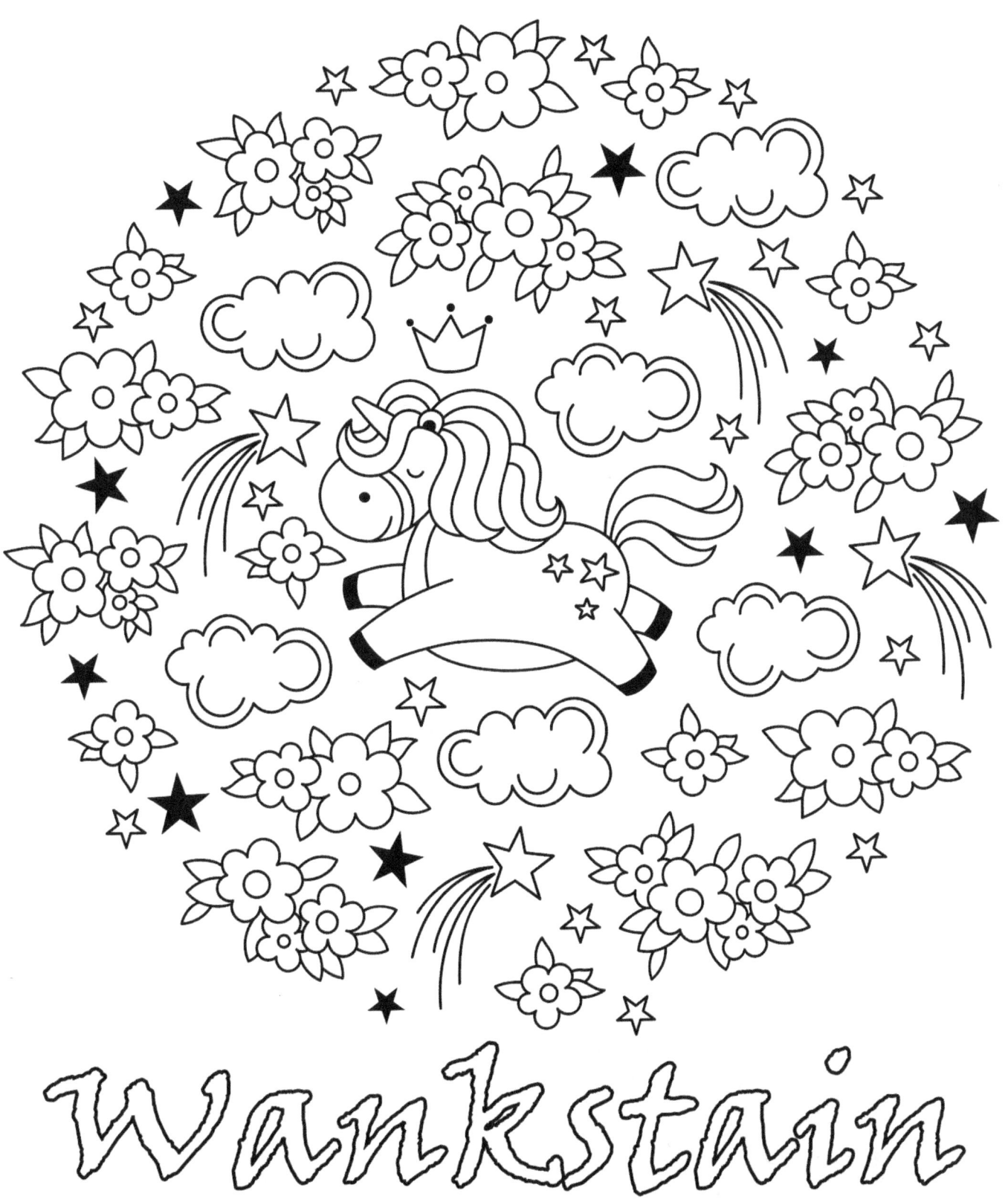

Wankstain

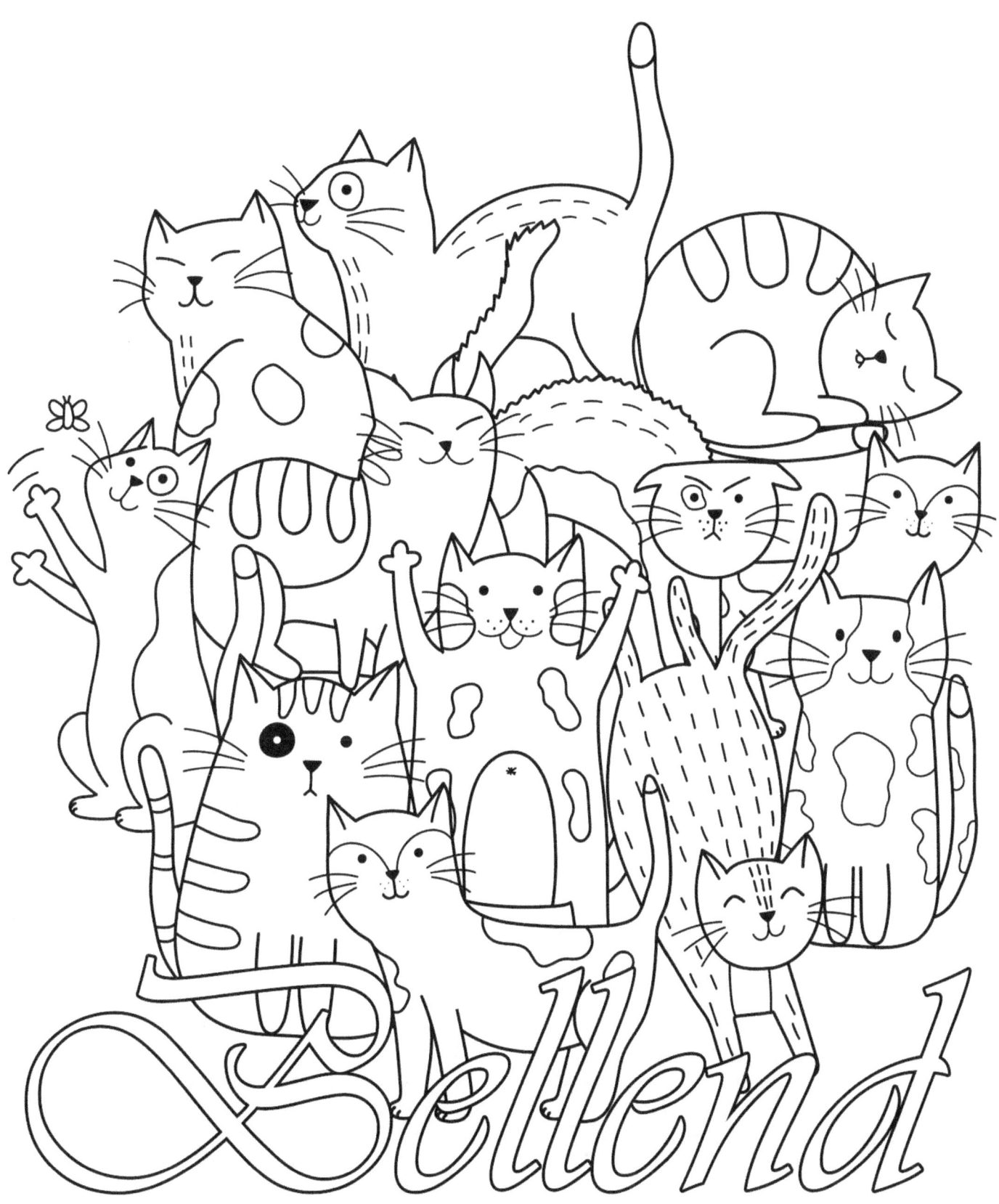

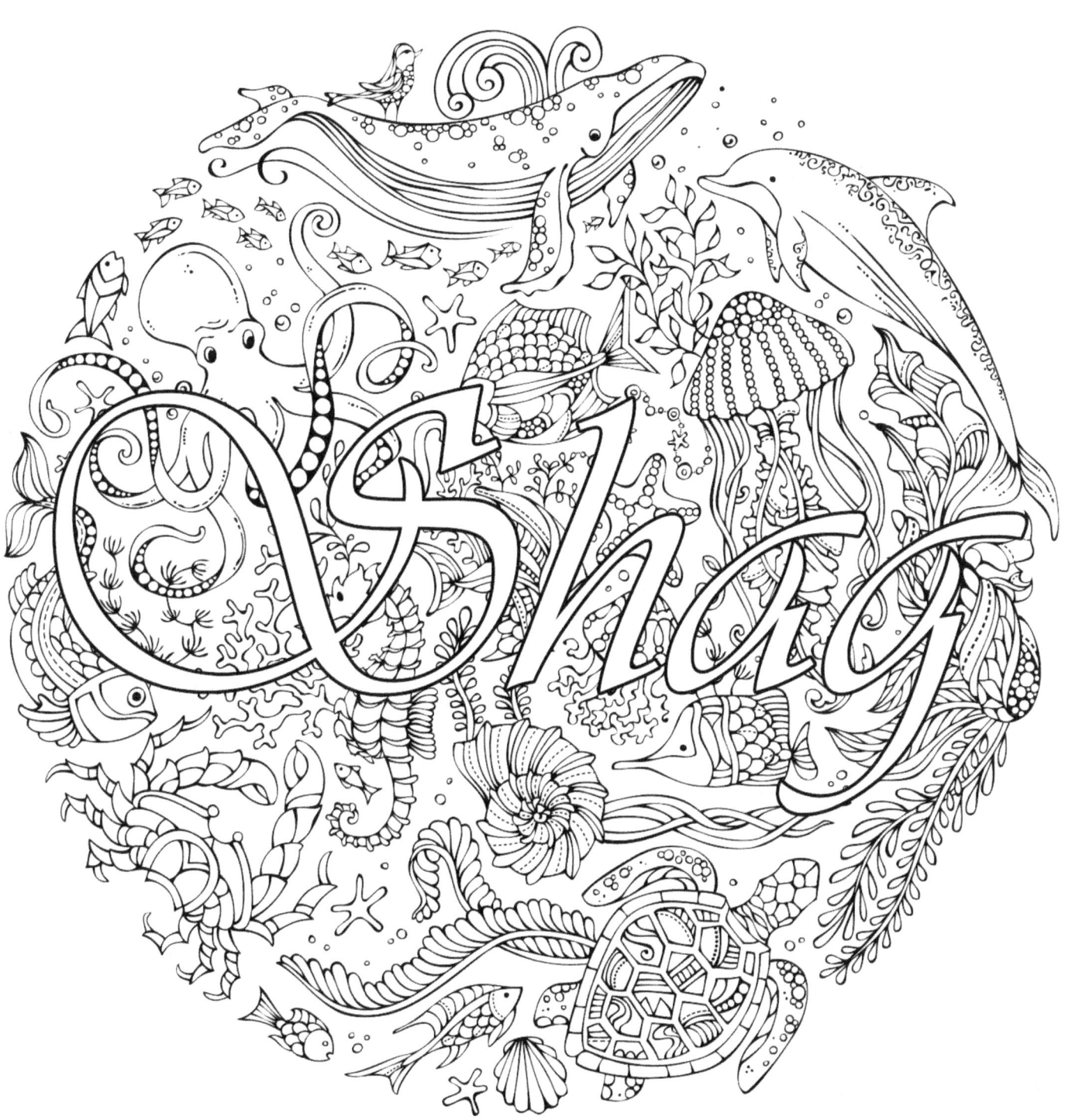

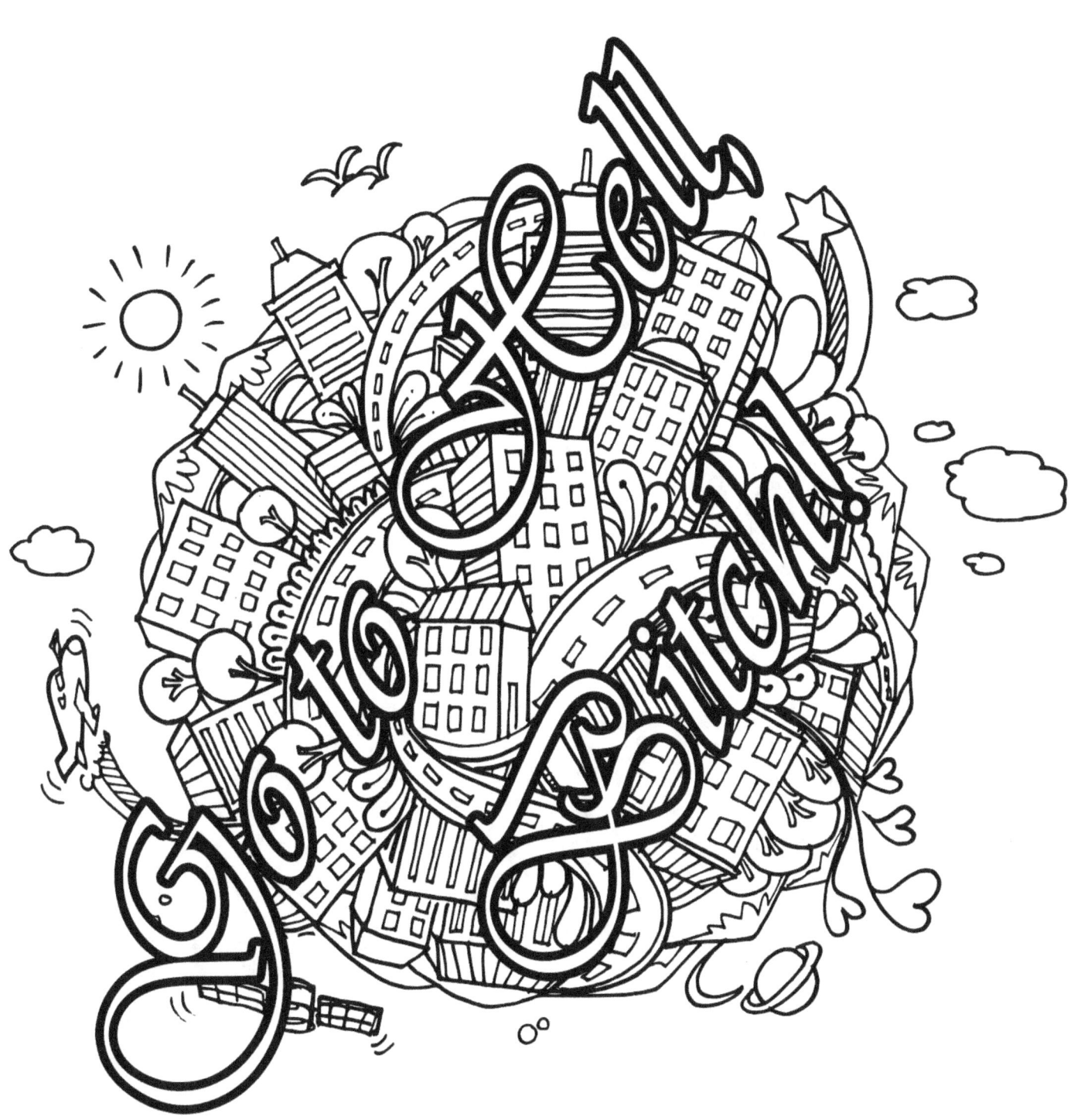

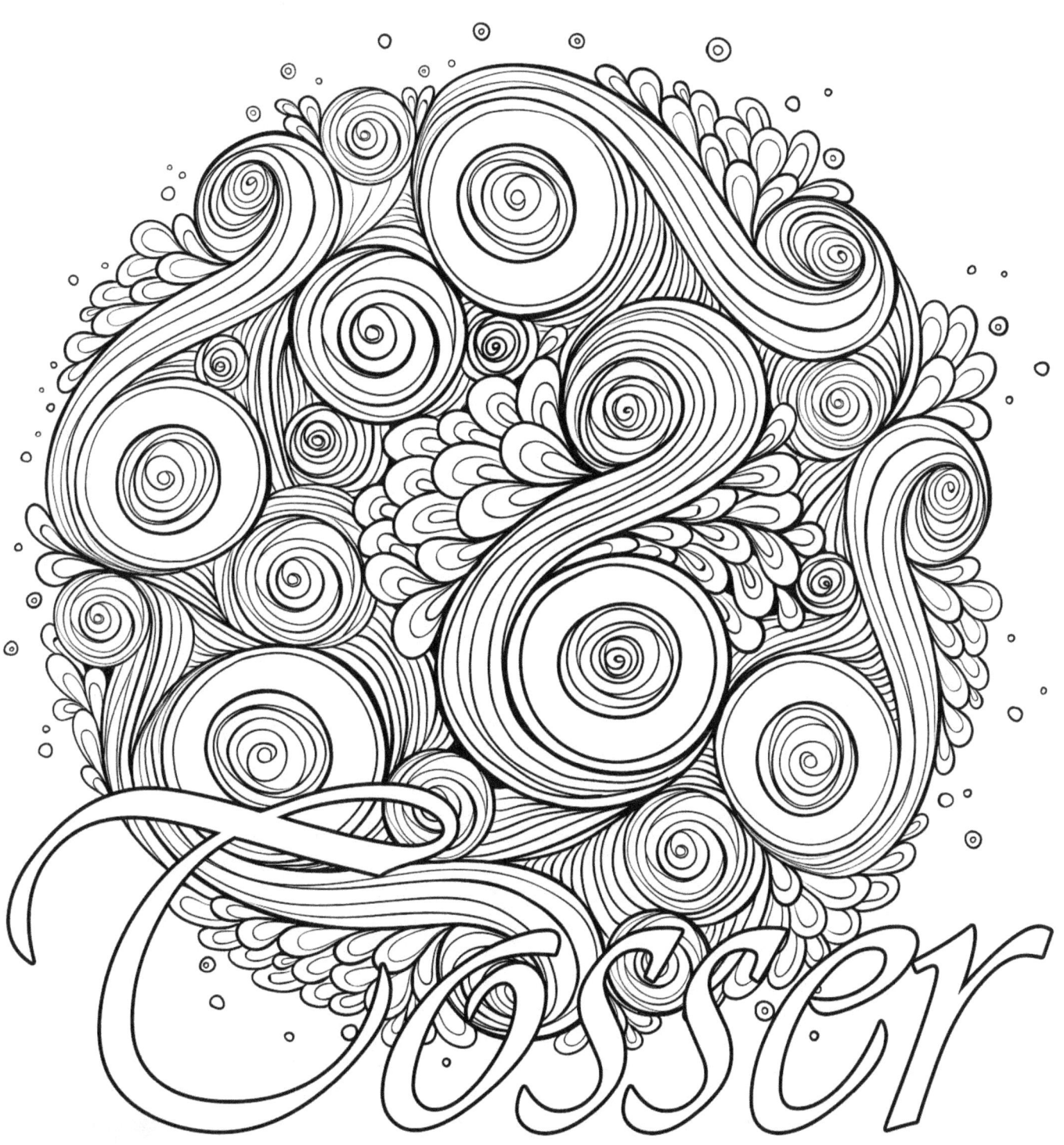

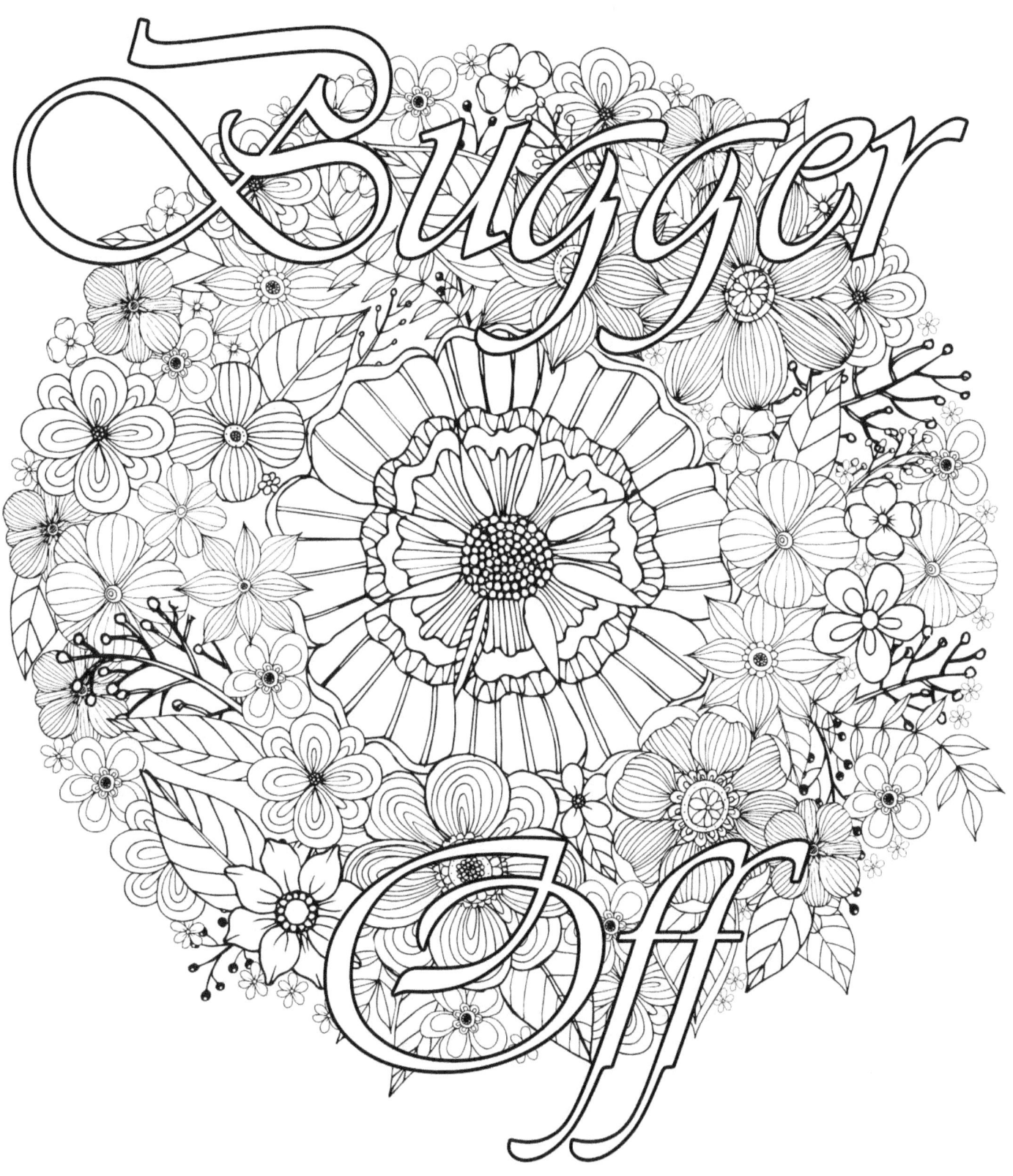

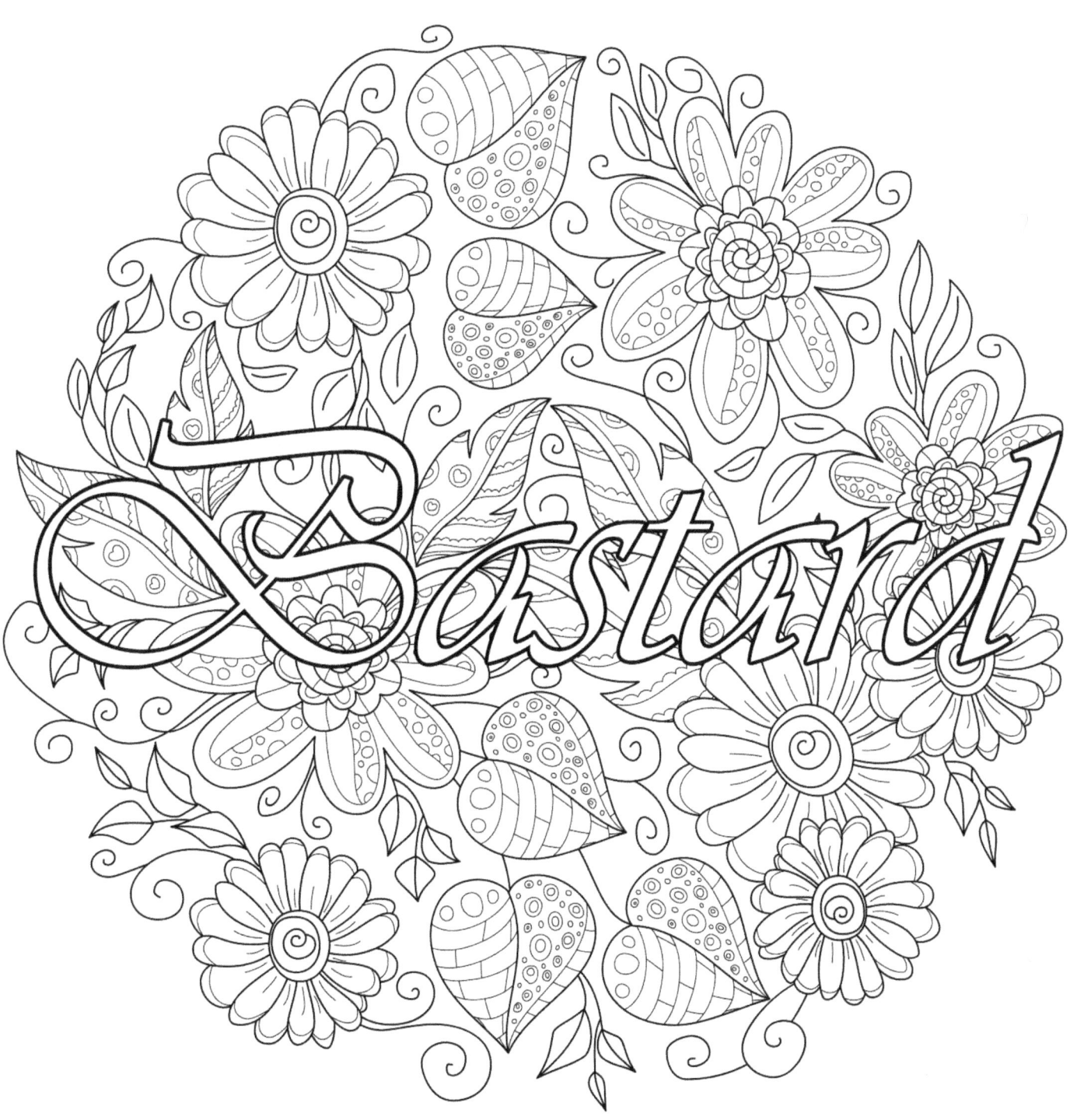

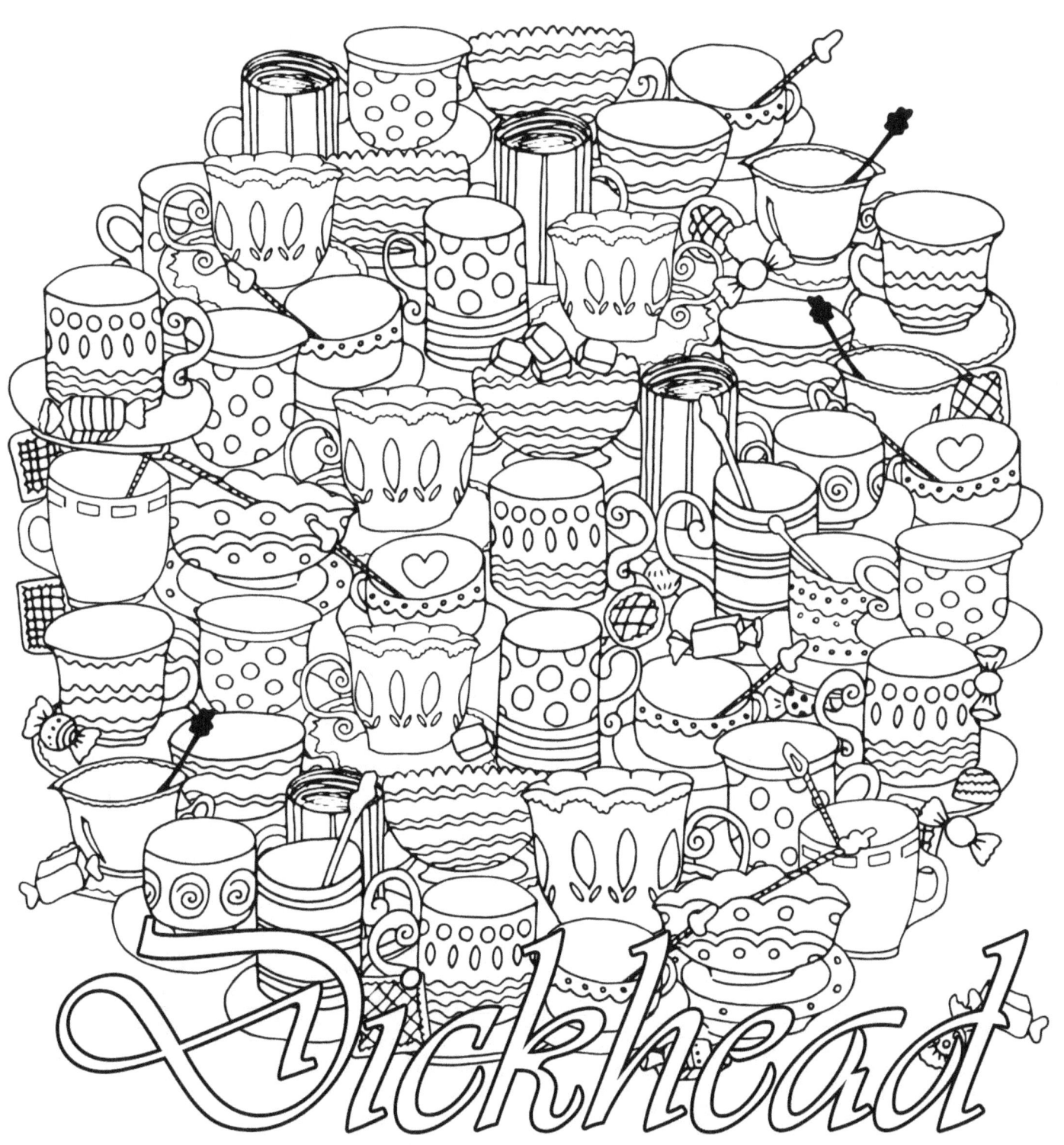

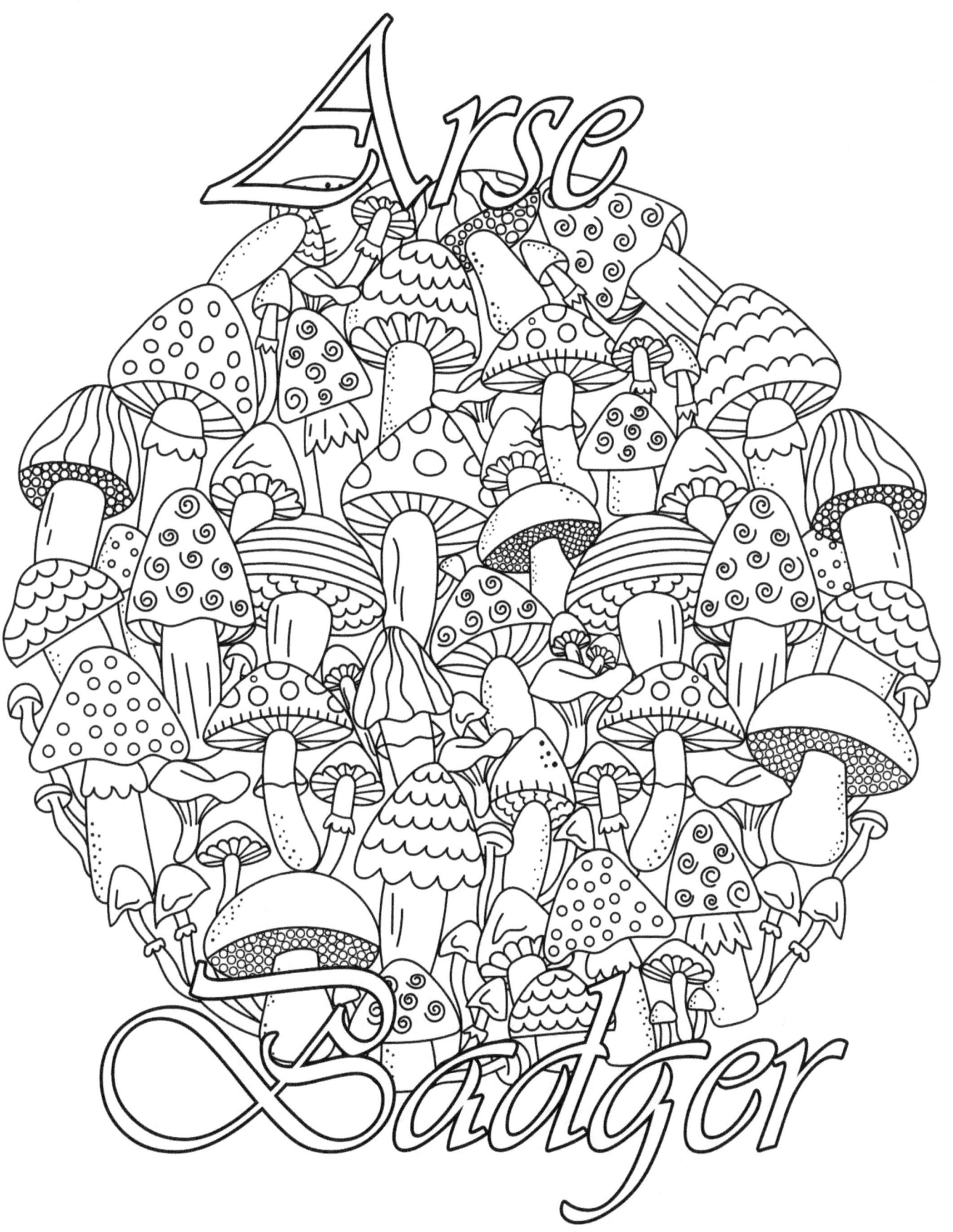

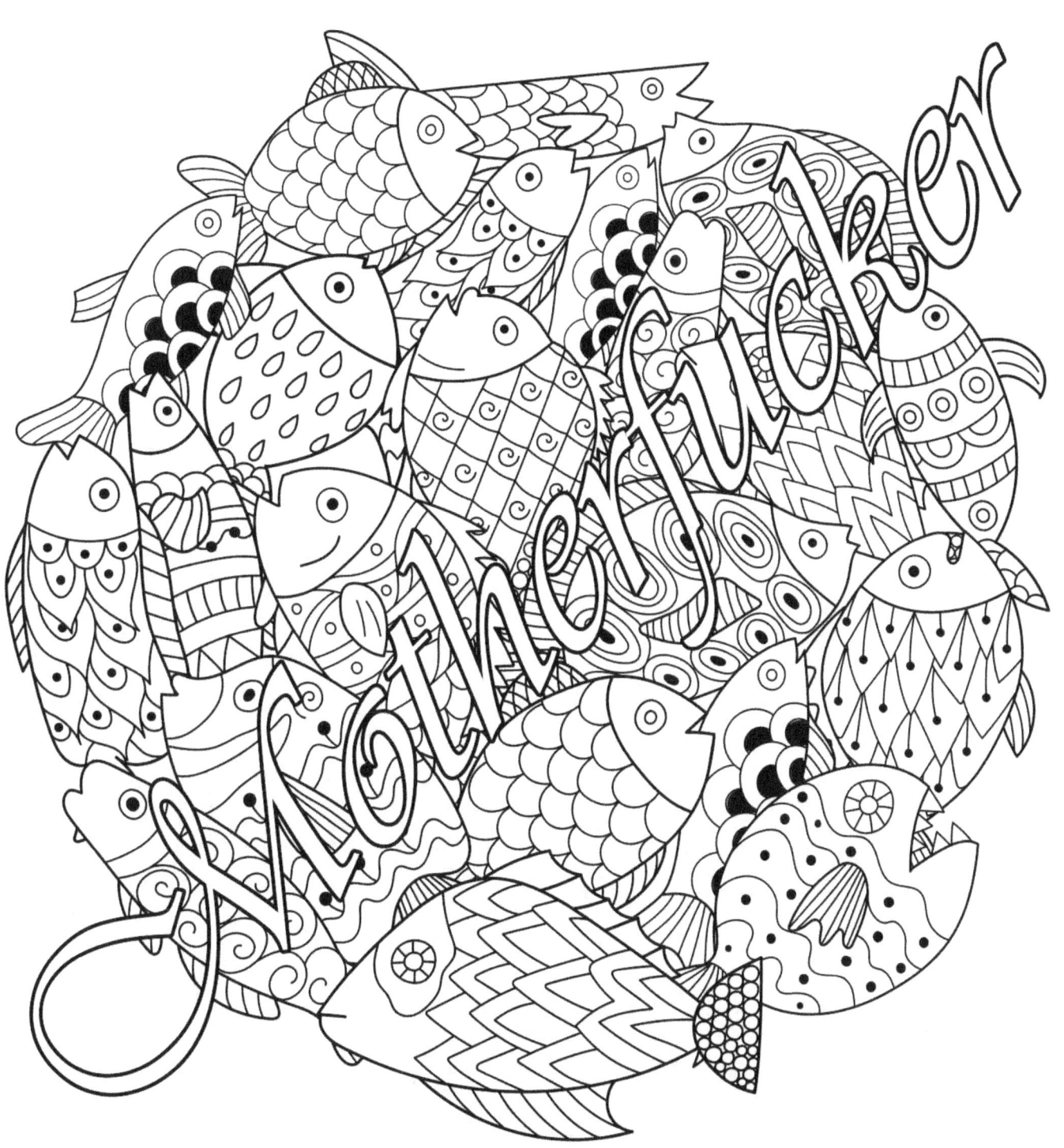

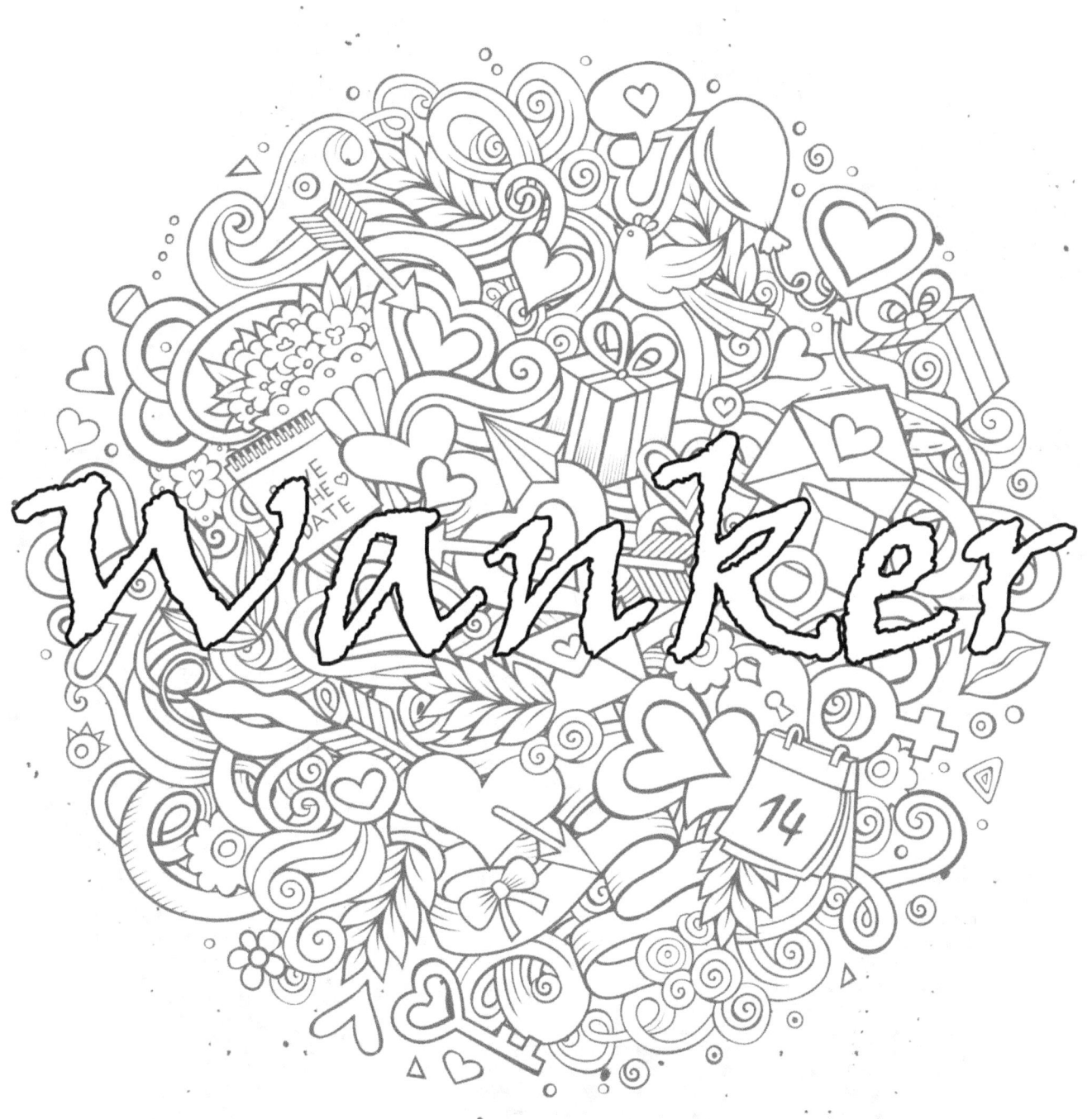

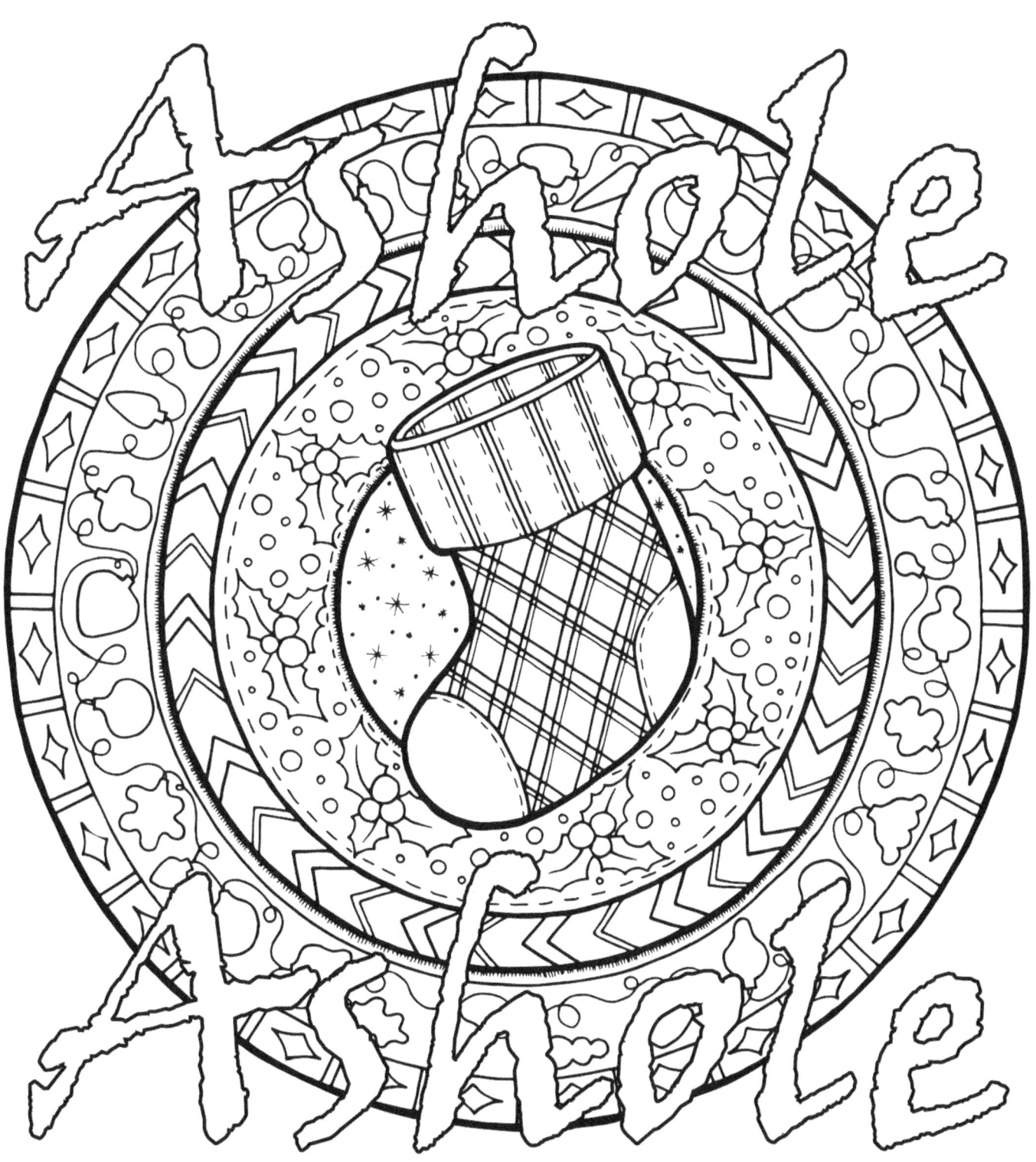